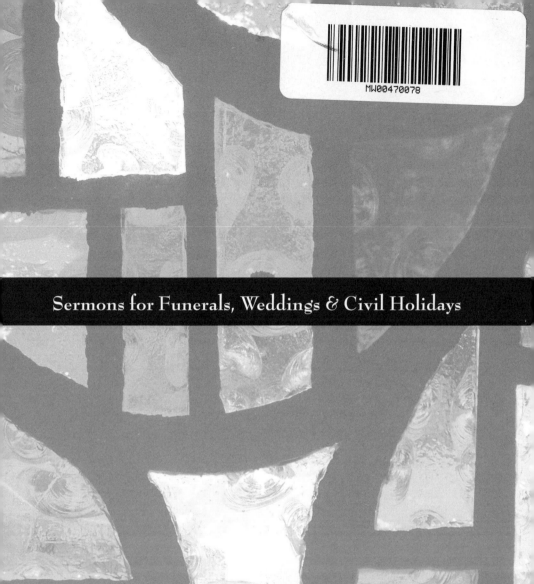

Sermons for Funerals, Weddings & Civil Holidays

Sermons for

Funerals, Weddings & Civil Holidays

Selections from
Concordia Pulpit
Resources

CONCORDIA PUBLISHING HOUSE · SAINT LOUIS

More Selections from Concordia Pulpit Resources

Sermons for Feasts, Festivals & Occasions (15-5104)

Sermons for Advent and Christmas (15-5105)

Sermons for Lent and Easter (15-5106)

Copyright © 2008 Concordia Publishing House
3558 S. Jefferson Ave., St. Louis, MO 63118-3968
1-800-325-3040 • www.cph.org

Manufactured in the United States of America

Library of Congress Cataloging-in-Publication Data

Sermons for funerals, weddings & civil holidays : selections from Concordia pulpit resources.
    p. cm.
    ISBN 978-0-7586-1377-6
    1. Funeral sermons. 2. Wedding sermons. 3. Festival-day sermons. 4.
    Lutheran Church—Sermons. I. Concordia pulpit resources II. Title:
    Sermons for funerals, weddings, and civil holidays.
BV4275.S48 2008
252'.1—dc22

    2007034382

1 2 3 4 5 6 7 8 9 10   17 16 15 14 13 12 11 10 09 08

Contents

Civil Holidays

Funerals

God Still Speaks in Storms

Job 1:6–22

Today our hearts go out to you, *(name)* and *(name)*, and to your family at your tremendous loss. The prayers and support of your fellow brothers and sisters in Christ are with you. We realize that nothing can take the pain away. No words from me or anyone else will release you from your sadness. We sympathize with you, we share Christ's love with you in word and action, and we trust that in His love you will find consolation, peace, and hope.

Not many years ago you went through a similar tragedy—the burial of another child. Sometimes we wonder why. We question God. "Why all this heartache to one individual, to one family? What is the reason? What good could possibly come of this sadness and overwhelming grief? What is the point of having faith if it seems there is no difference, if death and sadness enter equally into the lives of believers and unbelievers? Why, Lord? Why me?"

In our text, Job was a man blessed by God. He was a believer, and God loved and blessed him. Job had it all. He loved his wife. He had wonderful children— seven sons and three daughters. He owned land and cattle. He was wealthy and happy. In fact, Job was such a righteous man and good father that the Book of Job says: "He would rise early in the morning and offer burnt offerings according to the number of [all his children]. For Job said, 'It may be that my children have sinned, and cursed God in their hearts.' Thus Job did continually" (Job 1:5).

SATAN BRINGS THE STORM

Job loved his family. He loved God and served Him with loyalty and faithfulness. But that made Satan jealous. He wanted Job to follow his lead, not God's. As Satan watched Job's piety, he became angry and devised a plan to destroy him. He went to God and said, "Does Job fear God for no reason? Have You not put a hedge around him and his house and all that he has, on every side? You have blessed the work of his hands, and his possessions have increased in the land. But stretch out Your hand and touch all that he has, and he will curse You to Your face" (vv. 9–11). So God said to Satan, "Behold, all that he has is in your hand. Only against him do not stretch out your hand" (v. 12).

Scripture then records how Job lost everything in a day—his children, his cattle, his wealth. Desolation. Life was no longer a beautiful dream but had turned into a nightmare. Listen to Job's response. They are the words of a father grieving for his sons and his daughters: "Naked I came from my mother's womb, and naked shall I return. The LORD gave, and the LORD has taken away; blessed be the name of the LORD" (v. 21).

Job realized and uttered something profound about life. It is a point that we who are in the midst of living do not fully comprehend until loss comes. In one sense, nothing we have in this life is ours. What we think we own or call our own is only temporal. Job realized that life is not its trappings but is something more meaningful—a direction, a goal to which life leads, a place to which we aspire.

WHY A STORM?

As humans created in God's image, God has blessed us not only with the means to know, to learn, and to grow but also with the means to love. God gave to you the gift of loving *(name)* over these past *(number)* years. And you knew your child as someone who loved others. When God created Adam and Eve, He knew them and loved them. In return, they knew God and loved Him. The Book of Genesis tells us not only about how this world began, but it also tells us the answer to the world's greatest questions: "Why is there suffering in this world? Why the storm? Why death?"

Scripture records that Satan, too, was in the garden with Eve and Adam. Through temptation and doubt he led them into sin, and so death broke into the world. Adam and Eve would be the first parents to lose a child. That son was Abel, killed by his own brother, Cain. For the first time in this world, Adam and Eve saw and understood loss. Death hit home for them. Suddenly they saw the repercussion of the fall into sin. Imagine the hurt and sorrow Adam and Eve must have felt. What could comfort them? What could comfort Job and his wife in their loss? What can comfort you?

The Book of Job continues with Job's friends coming to comfort him. They do a poor job. Words and actions that lack understanding only drive Job into deeper despair. What could comfort him? The Book of Job records the account of a suffering believer desperately trying to make sense of it. This book deals with loss. Near the end of the book, Job, through a storm, hears God speak to him. And only after God speaks does Job find solace, peace, and a renewal of faith. God Himself comforted Job.

Perhaps a storm is what you, *(name)* and *(name)*, and your family feel you are going through. The weather may be nice, the sun shining, the birds singing, but within you a storm rages. Dark clouds of sadness and doubt loom over your hearts.

9

GOD STILL SPEAKS IN STORMS!

On Good Friday, God's Son died on a cross between two thieves. Scripture records that it was dark from noon until three o'clock. At that hour, Jesus spoke for the last time from His cross, "It is finished" (Jn 19:30). And so He died and was buried. But the tomb could not hold Him. Death could not keep Him. Easter came. The night of despair lifted; the choir of angels sang; the women at the tomb were met with joy and a message of hope. Christ was alive and appeared to His disciples. He said, "Peace be with you." And then Jesus "showed them His hands and His side. Then the disciples were glad when they saw the Lord. Jesus said to them again, 'Peace be with you. As the Father has sent Me, even so I am sending you.' And when He had said this, He breathed on them and said to them, 'Receive the Holy Spirit' " (Jn 20:19–22).

In the cleansing waters of Baptism, *(name)* received that same Spirit of God— the Spirit of faith and conviction in Jesus Christ as Lord. That faith was nurtured in him as a child, and he made a public profession of it in his confirmation.

We trust as believers that *(name)* has received the gift of faith, the everlasting crown of life. "Be faithful unto death, and I will give you the crown of life" (Rev 2:10). We trust that the Good Shepherd has guided His lamb through the valley of the shadow of death and that now *(name)* rests in the arms of the Savior who loves him. Now *(name)* can see and touch Jesus' nail wounds and pierced side. He can hear Christ say, "Peace be with you."

Christ is our comfort, our peace, our hope. *(Name)* and *(name)* and family, we entrust you into Christ's arms. God still speaks in storms! May His Spirit speak words of comfort and hope to your hearts. May your Shepherd's voice guide you through this storm of life as we, also, reach out to you with our Christian love and concern.

Rev. Grant T. Bode

Valleys and Mountaintops

Psalm 23; Revelation 7:9–17; John 10:14–16

Done

A coin has two sides. When you see one side, you don't see the other. In a similar way, the Bible gives us different sides or pictures of life. In Psalm 23, David portrays his life on earth as he is blessed and guided by God toward eternity in God's house. In Revelation 7 John points to life going on right now in heaven. Jesus tells us in John 10 that He is the link connecting the two realities, making them one reality with a great future.

In Psalm 23 David says, "Even though I walk through the valley of the shadow of death . . ." (v. 4). Our whole life is lived under the shadow of the enemy called death. Life has its joys and celebrations—marriages and births, graduations and promotions, barbecues and banquets. Yet it is also lived under a shadow, an overcast sky, the pall of death that lies ahead and won't go away even when we celebrate and laugh. Mark Twain said he would look in the paper each morning to make sure his name was not in the obituaries.

Caitland was a 5-year-old who contracted cancer. She went through radiation, chemotherapy, and surgery at a very young age. Whether we are 5, 15, or 50 years old, our bodies suffer the effects of living in a world that is in bondage to decay. God did not create this world and us to suffer in life. But ever since the transgression of Adam and Eve, which caused this world's fall into sin and death, human life—and indeed all life on earth—is lived out in the valley of the shadow of death. And when that shadow creeps over a loved one, and the enemy called death is allowed by God to swing his sickle, we who are left feel torn apart as one life is cut off from the rest of us who yet live. The hope of enjoying another day together and of doing things tomorrow is taken away. We feel a void, an emptiness.

The journey through the valley in shadow can seem like a lonesome walk that ends in isolation, defeat, and despair. But we who are in Christ have God's promise that we do not walk alone. With us walks a Friend who has trod this same path before us. He is the Good Shepherd who stands beside us today in our grief to give us guidance and direction. This Shepherd, whom David confessed as his Lord, deliberately strode into the shadowy valley. He left the brilliance of heaven, descended to earth, was conceived by the Holy Spirit of the Virgin Mary, and thus took upon Himself our human form and became one of us, though without sin. His perfect life was a display of God's merciful love and care for all people. He exercised His power to forgive sin and overcome death, disease, and the devil. He healed the sick, raised the dead, and cast out demons. His ministry led to the cross. There, the sinless Lamb of God was made to be sin for us. God laid on the Righteous One the iniquity of all humanity. He died in our place as a sacrifice pleasing to the Father. God accepted His fragrant offering, and Jesus was raised to life. After showing Himself alive to His apostles and followers, Jesus ascended to heaven and is now seated at the right hand of the Father. He has averted divine wrath from us and brought us grace.

David, the faithful king and a man after God's own heart, looks to the Lord as his ever-present Shepherd, who walks with him through the valley. "He makes me lie down in green pastures" (v. 2). He grants times of rest—physical, emotional, and spiritual. "He leads me beside still waters" (v. 2). A serene lake or the smooth flow of a meandering river can quiet jangled nerves and soothe a tormented and troubled heart. The Lord gives tranquility. He reminds us of the life-giving waters of Holy Baptism, poured over us in the name of the triune God, that give us peace with God and hope for eternity. As the funeral liturgy in *Lutheran Service Book* proclaims so clearly and powerfully, the sign of the cross made over the body in Baptism is repeated in the funeral service as a sign that the body washed in Baptism will be raised to new and eternal life in Christ. We are baptized into Christ's death, and into His resurrection.

"He restores my soul" (v. 3). There are times when we may feel alienated from God, as if He has forgotten us. Yet the Lord promises to restore and renew us. The Spirit poured out on us in Baptism renews our spirits. "He leads me in paths of righteousness for His name's sake" (v. 3). In our pilgrimage of life, our sin and the principalities and powers of this present darkness threaten to lead us astray. But our Lord is at work within us, moving us to will and to act according to His good pleasure. God guides us past danger and temptation in our daily life.

The psalmist's prayerful poem is directed toward Jesus Christ, the Good Shepherd. As we are gathered here in His name, He is present to hear our pleas for help in the hour of mourning. "Call upon Me in the day of trouble," He said, promising, "I will deliver you" (Ps 50:15). Again He said, "Come to Me, all who labor and are heavy laden, and I will give you rest" (Mt 11:28). We are not alone as we traverse the valley of the shadow. The Lord Jesus has walked it before and is walking it with us today.

Let's change scenes now. We move from the valley to the mountaintop, to the other side of the coin, where people are living with God in the next life. John takes us there.

We see a great multitude that no one can count, from every tribe and nation, people and language. They are standing before the throne and in front of the Lamb. And who are these people, this great multitude? They are those who have come out of the great tribulation—that is, out of the sufferings of this life, through the valley of the shadow of death. They are those who have passed through and are now on the other side of the valley. We cannot see them, except in memory. But through the apostle John, God has given us a vision of their joyful glory. Our loved one has laid aside the burdens and battles, the stresses and strains of valley-walking. Our loved one has joined the great multitude in the throne room of heaven.

What enables these multitudes to stand in the unveiled presence of God? Those who enter before the throne "have washed their robes and made them white in the blood of the Lamb" (Rev 7:14). They have been washed in Baptism. That washing applies to them the cleansing power of the shed blood of Jesus Christ. They have been given faith by the power of the Holy Spirit poured out on them, and with that faith they have received the forgiveness of sins achieved by Jesus on the cross for all humankind. They have received the Savior and His new resurrection life. He died in the valley that they might live on the mountain.

If there were a window into heaven, we might see *(name)* standing there among the white-robed saints. She believed in the Lord Jesus, the only Savior from sin. Her robes were washed in the blood of Jesus. Upon death she came out of the valley of tribulation into eternal life on the mountaintop. And these white-robed saints are singing with special, sevenfold exhilaration: "Blessing and glory and wisdom and thanksgiving and honor and power and might be to our God forever and ever! Amen" (Rev 7:12).

They sing because the Lamb at the center of the throne is their Shepherd. He leads them to springs of living water. He wipes away every tear from their eyes. The process of dying produces many tears, both by those who are passing onward and by those left behind. But Jesus, the Good Shepherd, will wipe away all tears with His love. Those before the throne sing because they have been freed from all pain and sorrow. Their place in glory is secure forever.

We can join them in singing. By God's grace, our destination is with the white-robed saints. We are confident in God's promise that soon we, too, will join all of God's saints in glory and remain with them forever and ever. We look to Jesus, the pioneer and perfecter of our faith. His position is before the throne of His Father as our advocate, our mediator. He pleads for us. He has prepared a place for us among the throng gathered before the Father.

We started in the valley and then moved to the mountaintop. Now we come to Jesus' words in the Gospel of John. He has a word about the present age in which we live. Jesus said, "I have other sheep that are not of this fold. I must bring them also, and they will listen to My voice. So there will be one flock, one shepherd" (Jn 10:16). When He first spoke those words, His apostles and most of His followers were Jewish believers. Jesus spoke of a time when many from the rest of the world's nations—Gentiles—would be brought into His flock. Jesus removed the wall dividing Jews from Gentiles. In this age of the Christian Church, all people—

of every nationality, ethnic origin, race, and language—are welcome in the flock of His followers.

In the Creed, we confess that we believe in the one holy catholic/Christian Church. That is an article of faith rather than something we can observe now. At present, we see divisions in the Church with many denominations and conflicting opinions. While there may not be external concord and harmony, all in Christ comprise one flock with one Shepherd. The apostle Paul reminds us: "There is one body and one Spirit—just as you were called to the one hope that belongs to your call—one Lord, one faith, one baptism, one God and Father of all, who is over all and through all and in all" (Eph 4:4–6).

(Name) has that one true faith in the Lord. On earth she listened to the Shepherd's voice. We can look forward to seeing her again, since the saints alive on earth and the white-robed saints of heaven will one day be together in a new heaven and earth united under Christ, the Head (Eph 1:10).

Jesus looks forward to the time of His return. He will come from heaven (1 Thess 4:16; Rev 21:2) with all His holy angels. In a moment, in a twinkling of an eye, at the sound of the last trumpet, the dead will be raised with imperishable and immortal bodies (1 Cor 15:52), and all those still in the vanishing valley will also be changed. Even those who have shut their ears to the Savior's voice will be raised, but their eternal fate is torment in body and soul in the lake of fire (Jn 5:28–29; Rev 20:14–15). But all of us who are in Christ Jesus will be gathered into one flock, united with our Shepherd and Lamb, Jesus.

We have covered a lot of "ground" this morning, walking through the valley, rising to the mountaintops, and glimpsing the future in Christ. I pray that these words of the Lord may encourage you in your living faith and also in your hope that we will all be together with the Lord Jesus forever.

Rev. Raymond L. Schiefelbein

The Beauty of This Day

Ecclesiastes 3:1–2a, 11a

Today does not seem beautiful. At first glance there is nothing beautiful about today. It is a day of mourning and great personal loss. Weeping seems more appropriate than the appreciation of beauty. In no way do we discount the sorrow of the day nor the tears that are shed, for the sense of loss you are experiencing is real. St. Paul instructs us, "Rejoice with those who rejoice, weep with those who weep" (Rom 12:15). Therefore, today we mingle our tears with yours as we are privileged to share the burden of your sorrow. After all, the years of shared living are now abruptly ended.

How sweetly and yet painfully do you remember the beginning of the new love that began your marriage together? How bittersweet are your memories of sharing in the making of a new home or of bringing the God-given blessing of children into the world? How fondly did you embrace the comfort of long-lived companionship that grew more deeply with the passing of the years together? And yes, the time near the end when disease forced a final sharing of life's experience together. Death never seems appropriate at all, let alone beautiful. Rather, when we see death or experience it at close hand, we associate it with something bad, ugly, and morbid. In many ways, that is precisely what death is like.

And now, in addition to the sense of loss, there is also the uncertainty of the future that lies ahead. Yes, weeping is certainly an appropriate response in the face of grief. Jesus, too, wept at the death of a dear friend, Lazarus. Our Lord knows precisely the sorrow you feel this day and shares it with you.

But our mourning today is not the end of it all. Our text says plainly that there is more to life and death than futility, pain, and suffering. If we are to be ready to meet either life or death, we must see the beauty of God's Son, Jesus Christ, for only in Him can we find the true meaning and comfort we seek on this day of sadness.

IN CHRIST, EVEN A DAY LIKE THIS BECOMES A THING OF BEAUTY

Today we see the beautiful fulfillment of your loved one's Christian faith. God's promise of eternal life through Christ has been fulfilled for *(name)*. While we yet struggle with the pain of the moment, for *(name)* God's promise that "all things work together for good" (Rom 8:28) is now a reality.

Like the rest of us, *(name)* would be quick to sing the praises of God, who took a *(man/woman)* who was a sinner and transformed *(him/her)* into a child of the living God. Like all of us, *(name)* had been estranged from God, divorced from our Creator because that is the way we are conceived and born. With *(name)*, we all must confess with David, "Behold, I was brought forth in iniquity, and in sin did my mother conceive me" (Ps 51:5). But God would not let us perish. Consider the beauty of what the Father accomplished through His Son. Through Christ's atoning sacrifice, the stain of our sin, which disqualified us from life with God, was removed. As St. Paul puts it, "For our sake He made Him to be sin who knew no sin, so that in Him we might become the righteousness of God" (2 Cor 5:21).

The cross on which our Lord gave His life for us was not, at first glance, a thing of beauty, but it is to us now. This ugly instrument of Roman execution has become the very symbol of the Christian faith. Now it is prominently seen on Christian churches throughout the world. It is the sign of our hope, our life, and the beauty of our salvation.

Also, a hole in the ground is rarely considered a thing of beauty, much less a rock-hewn tomb. But on this day of mourning, let us remember the resplendent beauty of an empty tomb. Its occupant could not be held by the constraints of death. On this day, of all days, let us remember the beauty of the empty tomb and know that we have not seen the last of *(name)*! For as Christ has risen from the dead so, too, will all who have been buried with Christ in Baptism be raised to life in Christ's resurrection. Yes, today, despite our tears, we can see the beauty of the grave because we know that the day will come when that grave will be as empty as Christ's was. Through the beauty of Christ's empty grave we know that death cannot, will not, shall not have the last word today or any other day!

And what of your future, the days and weeks and years ahead that you thought you would experience with your beloved *(name)*? What will they be like? This much is certain: you are not going into the future alone! God will walk with you to bear you up when your sorrow revisits you in the days ahead. The great Christian apologist C. S. Lewis once said, "God whispers to us in our pleasure, but He shouts to us in our pain." God does not promise that the days will be easy, but He does promise to give us the strength we will need to face each new day. With St. Paul we hear Christ's voice saying, "My grace is sufficient for you, for My power is made perfect in weakness" (2 Cor 12:9). Cling to the precious means of grace, God's Word and Sacraments, for they alone can strengthen and bring joy even in the face of death and in the hardships of life. Lean on the community of Christ, God's people, who will comfort you and share your burdens as well as your joys. Most important, cling to Christ Jesus, under the shadow of whose cross both life and death have become instruments of His grace.

—*Rev. Richard A. Bolland*

The Best Is Yet to Come

Ecclesiastes 3:11a

Our hearts are very heavy this morning. We are shocked at the sudden death of Charles. Our pain is very deep. We are left numb and maybe even confused. Why did this have to happen to such a fine young person? He was a beloved husband, father, and son. His family meant so much to him. He was always willing to help wherever he could. He was a caring person to all, a true servant of God.

What do we do now? Where do we go to find some meaning, some hope in all of this? There is a beautiful story recorded in John 6. Jesus, who is preaching and teaching to a large crowd about being sent by God, proclaims that He is the true source of life. He is the "bread of life." Some of the people in the crowd couldn't accept this. They walked out on Jesus, and soon others followed. They could no longer believe in Him.

Jesus turned to His disciples and asked, "Do you want to go away as well?" Peter responded, "Lord, to whom shall we go? You have the words of eternal life, and we have believed, and have come to know, that You are the Holy One of God" (Jn 6:67–69). Peter was saying in effect, "You are God! You are the One who has the whole world in Your hands. You are the One who does not make mistakes!"

Our God speaks through His prophet Isaiah, "My thoughts are not your thoughts, neither are your ways My ways, declares the LORD. For as the heavens are higher than the earth, so are My ways higher than your ways and My thoughts than your thoughts" (Is 55:8–9).

And in the New Testament our Lord speaks through the apostle Peter, "Beloved, do not be surprised at the fiery trial when it comes upon you to test you, as though something strange were happening to you. But rejoice insofar as you share Christ's sufferings" (1 Pet 4:12–13).

Nothing is happenstance for us Christians. Nothing occurred to Charles until it first passed our Father's heart. He sifted through it all and then decided what He would permit or send or discard. Our loving God knows what is best for us in accordance to His eternal plan. The writer of the Epistle to the Hebrews says, "[God] disciplines us for our good, that we may share His holiness" (Heb 12:10).

This terrible tragedy reminds us yet again how helpless we are sometimes and, therefore, how utterly dependent we are on God's love and power. It can help us to be more open to the workings of the Holy Spirit, of being drawn closer to our heavenly Father. I would think Charles was drawn closer to his Lord once he learned about his seizures. Yet our Lord started working on Charles' heart long before that. The Holy Spirit came into his life when he was baptized as an infant. Then and there God claimed Charles as His very own. The Holy Spirit worked in his heart every time he read his Bible or heard God's Word in worship. The Spirit worked when Charles meditated on the mysteries of God. The Spirit moved Charles to serve his Lord faithfully through the ministry of Hope Lutheran Church.

Sometimes, in grace and love, God permits or prolongs illness for the purpose of bringing us to the Spirit-given acceptance that He is Lord of all—including life and death—to equip us to live as disciples of Jesus Christ.

Once we have learned the lessons He wants us to learn and know, once He accomplishes what He wants with us in His love, then God moves us to experience even greater blessings from Him. The greatest blessing is that which God has already given to Charles—the gift of eternal life. Jesus made this possible by giving His life on the cross. He paid for our failures and sins. He came back to life again, conquering death, our greatest enemy. Our resurrected Lord said, "Because I live, you also will live" (Jn 14:19). Charles surely heard our Lord say to him on Friday, "Come, you who are blessed by My Father, inherit the kingdom prepared for you from the foundation of the world" (Mt 25:34).

We rejoice with Charles, but we hurt for ourselves. God will be with you in the coming days and years, filling your void with His gentle presence and peace. He will give you guidance and strength to meet each day. Jesus said, "In My Father's house are many rooms. If it were not so, would I have told you that I go to prepare a place for you? And if I go and prepare a place for you, I will come again and will take you to Myself, that where I am you may be also" (Jn 14:2–3). Jesus has prepared a place for us. He will come back and take us with Him. We will be reunited with Charles. We shall see him again. The best is yet to come, as the writer of Ecclesiastes says, "He has made everything beautiful in its time" (Eccl 3:11). To this we echo St. Paul, "Thanks be to God, who gives us the victory through our Lord Jesus Christ" (1 Cor 15:57).

Rev. Daniel J. Teuscher

Lifted in Love

Isaiah 40:28–31

To many people there is no grander sight than that of an eagle in flight. As they watch a majestic bird soar, strong and free, their own spirits seem to be lifted. Their hearts are encouraged. When our heavenly Father spoke to the children of Israel through the prophet Isaiah, this is the type of picture He wanted them to see. Their spirits were low, and they were weary, for they had lost their homes and homeland. I would like you to see the same picture today as you mourn the loss of John, your loving husband, father, and friend.

God Enables Us, by Faith in Christ Jesus, to Soar as on Eagles' Wings

Before we soar heavenward like eagles, however, the unhappy reality is that life in a world stained by sin often leaves us tired, weary, weak, stumbling, and fallen, to paraphrase Isaiah. Although that is not a pretty picture, it is realistic. Young men do become old, energetic people lose their stamina, healthy people lose their vitality, graceful people stumble and fall. Sadly, we saw these things take place in John's final months and days. We see them happen in our own lives when we, like the Israelites, give in to disappointment, discouragement, and defeat.

At Home but Called Away

Thankfully, though we sometimes forget God's promise of deliverance, He never forgets us. Although many of us have seen pictures of a huge eagle's nest high in the branches of a tree or in the crag of a cliff, few of us have glimpsed inside. Those who study eagles have learned that when a mother eagle builds her nest, she starts with thorns, broken branches, sharp rocks, and a number of other items that seem entirely unsuitable for the project. But she doesn't stop there. She then lines the nest with a thick padding of feathers, fur, and other soft materials, which make it comfortable for her children when they hatch. By the time the young birds are able to fly, the comfort of the nest makes them reluctant to leave. Soon thereafter, however, the mother eagle begins "stirring the nest." With her strong talons, she starts to pull apart and remove the soft materials, allowing the sharp objects to come to the surface. As more of the bedding gets plucked away, the nest, which was for a while a comfortable home, becomes increasingly uncomfortable to the point that the young eagles are ready to leave home and soar to a new home in a higher place.

With tender words Isaiah reminds us that God does something similar for us. No, He does not intentionally cause us pain, but He does use weariness, weakness, and tiredness to remind us that heaven is our home, not earth. It is our heavenly Father's intention that after we have lived our lives, loved our spouses, nurtured our children and grandchildren, worked our craft, served our country, improved our neighborhoods, strengthened our churches—just as John did so well for so long—we, too, are ready to leave our earthly homes to be carried in the arms of the angels to our heavenly home, which is, after all, the beautiful paradise Jesus has prepared for us.

READY TO BE LIFTED IN LOVE

One day a Kansas farmer found a baby eagle in one of his fields. The poor young eagle was not in good condition, so the farmer took it to his home to nurse it back to health. Over the next few weeks, the young eagle improved, and the farmer put it in with the young chicks in his chicken coop. Although the eagle gained strength and stamina, it was obvious that the bird was beginning to grow listless and seemed to be losing its spark for life. The farmer feared the young eagle might die after all, despite his best intentions. A possible solution came to mind. He put the eagle into his pickup truck and drove west to Colorado. When he arrived at the eastern edge of the Rockies, the farmer carried the young bird into the foothills. Then he held the eagle in his arms and pointed its head toward the mountaintops, where the wind was blowing. Another eagle cried out as it traced the currents of the mountain winds. A shudder coursed through the young eagle's body, and it spread its wings. As a new strength seemed to surge through the bird, it leaped into the air, caught a strong breeze, and soared into the sky. With a tear of both sorrow and joy, the farmer listened as the eagle cried out what seemed to be a farewell and soared upward to become the bird it was destined to be.

Our heavenly Father has done that for us. By Jesus' sacrificial death on the cross and His triumphant resurrection, sin and death no longer ground us. By faith in Jesus—faith like John exemplified so well for us—we are lifted as on wings of an eagle to the heights of heaven. That is true for John, and it will be true for you and me. Heaven is our home, and our heavenly Father has done everything necessary to make it possible for us to be with Him. Charles Wesley said it well in the Easter hymn "Christ the Lord Is Risen Today." *(Recite LSB 469:2–5.)*

Today, take heart in John's life and love. And, more than that, take heart in the strength of the Lord who lifts us on eagles' wings and loves us eternally!

Rev. David R. Zachrich

Soaring with the Everlasting God

Isaiah 40:28–31

Dear family and friends of Karl, especially you, his mom and dad, brothers and grandparents. Along with Job we say, "The LORD gave, and the LORD has taken away; blessed be the name of the LORD" (Job 1:21).

Dear parents, the Lord gave Karl to you to love and to nurture his faith in Jesus as his Savior. It was your privilege to raise Karl, and all your children, in the training and instruction of the Lord. You faithfully listened to God's invitation in His Word when He said, "Let the children come to Me, and do not hinder them, for to such belongs the kingdom of God" (Lk 18:16). You were obedient to the command of our Lord to make disciples for Him, having your children baptized in the name of the Father and of the Son and of the Holy Spirit.

In addition, you taught them yourselves and brought them to God's house where your Christian family assisted you in teaching them what God has commanded us. You saw to it that your children received biblical instruction leading to confirmation. Karl personally and publicly affirmed his Christian faith at his confirmation. And you continued to encourage, admonish, and train him in the way of godliness and faith. The Lord gave Karl to you to prepare him for life with God, and now the Lord has taken him to be with Himself.

GOD'S WAYS ARE NOT ALWAYS OUR WAYS

We don't understand God's ways, but we do understand and believe God's promises, which He spoke through His apostle, saying, "Neither death nor life, nor angels nor rulers, nor things present nor things to come, nor powers, nor height nor depth, nor anything else in all creation, will be able to separate us from the love of God in Christ Jesus our Lord" (Rom 8:38–39).

We believe God's promises when He says, "Whoever believes and is baptized will be saved" (Mk 16:15), and again, "He who began a good work in you will bring it to completion at the day of Jesus Christ" (Phil 1:6), and yet again, "We would rather be away from the body and at home with the Lord" (2 Cor 5:8).

Your goal for your children has been to prepare them for their heavenly home. For Karl, by God's grace, that goal has now been completed. And so we can say with you, "Blessed be the name of the LORD" (Job 1:21).

What you weren't prepared for, and who of us would be, was for your first-born son to be taken to heaven so soon! Our hearts ache, and we grieve with you over the sudden and accidental death of your son. We can't find words to convey to you how deeply we hurt because of your loss and how much we want to help and support you in this time of your need. Although we don't have words that are adequate, God does. The word that I would like for you to hear from God in your grief and to remember for your comfort is recorded in Is 40:28–31:

> Have you not known? Have you not heard? The LORD is the everlasting God, the Creator of the ends of the earth. He does not faint or grow weary; His understanding is unsearchable. He gives power to the faint, and to him who has no might He increases strength. Even youths shall faint and be weary, and young men shall fall exhausted; but they who wait for the LORD shall renew their strength; they shall mount up with wings like eagles; they shall run and not be weary; they shall walk and not faint.

These are words that I think Karl, with his love for flying, would have particularly appreciated.

Have you ever watched an eagle soar? It's a beautiful sight. If you pay careful attention, the eagle's flight is quite instructive. Eagles are powerful birds, yet they don't soar by the power of their wings. They are able to soar because of the current of the wind. That's why they don't get tired; they aren't relying on their strength, their resources. If they did, they would grow weary and fall to the ground. Instead, they rely on the wind currents to keep them aloft. In the same way, God wants us to rely on Him and His Spirit so that we can soar, not only in this life but also in the life that is to come. He wants us to soar with Him, the everlasting God.

Isaiah wrote in the words immediately before our text, "Why do you say, O Jacob, and speak, O Israel, 'My way is hidden from the LORD, and my right is disregarded by my God'?" (Is 40:27). It's so easy at a time such as this, when we are trying to make sense out of such a shocking and tragic accident, to think that either the Lord doesn't know what's going on in your life or He simply doesn't care. We know that is not the case. I can't explain to you, I can't understand myself, why such tragedies happen.

THE LORD KNOWS THE HURT OF HIS PEOPLE

What I do know is this: the Lord is not unaware of you or your sorrow. He is not uncaring. He cries every tear with you. Who would know better than our heavenly Father what it is like to lose a beloved Son? He sent His own Son into this sinful world, knowing what that would mean. There was no other way for sinners such as you and me to be rescued from eternal destruction. We needed a sinless Substitute. Yet no one but God Himself is without sin in this creation ruined by the disobedience of Adam and Eve. Thus out of His great love for us, God sent forth His beloved and only Son to our world. The Son of God humbled Himself, and by the power of the Holy Spirit was planted as a seed in the womb of a virgin. He was born of a human mother, Mary, and like us was subject to God's perfect Law. But unlike us, Jesus obeyed the Law perfectly so that He might redeem us from the curse of the Law. Sin's curse brings death. Jesus willingly took your curse and mine to that accursed tree of the cross and died there to take death away forever.

Did the Father not know what was happening? Didn't He care? Of course He knew and cared excruciatingly. Then why did He do it? If we didn't have a sinless Substitute, then death would have won, and the continuation of life here in this world would have been pointless. God gave His beloved Son to death because He loved us and wanted us to have life with Him now and forever.

But that's not all. Three days later, our heavenly Father raised Jesus from the grave, for death could not hold Him. Now He promises us, and all who believe in His Son, that those who are joined with Him by faith are heirs of the same resurrection, the same hope, the same new and eternal life that Jesus has. All of this is guaranteed by the resurrection of Jesus Christ. Because of Christ's resurrection, we can rejoice in the resurrection of the dead and the life of the world to come.

Facing the Future

The question remains: "How do we go on from here? Where will we find the strength?" Our strength is not found within ourselves or our own resolve or determination to continue with life. Instead, God says, "Lift up your eyes on high and see. . . . The Lord is the everlasting God, the Creator of the ends of the earth. . . . He gives power to the faint, and to him who has no might He increases strength. . . . They who wait for the Lord shall renew their strength; they shall mount up with wings like eagles; they shall run and not be weary; they shall walk and not faint" (Is 40:26, 28–29, 31).

If you have been given faith, then you have also been given wings! So, my dear friends, spread your wings, and know that the Lord lifts you in His hands. Don't depend on your own resources. Trust His good and gracious will for you! Believe Him! Soar! Sail on the wind that the Spirit provides in His Word and you will not grow weary, you will not be faint. Those who hope in the Lord will renew their strength as they soar with our everlasting God.

Rev. Alvin H. Lange

You Are Mine

Isaiah 49:16

There is a story in the Bible of one man who never died (Gen 5:24). His name was Enoch. Scripture says that God translated him directly from life on earth to the presence of God in heaven (Heb 11:5).

A little girl was once asked to tell the story of Enoch. She said, "Well, Enoch and God were good friends. And they used to take long walks in Enoch's garden. One day God said, 'Enoch, you look tired. Why don't you come to My place and stay and rest awhile?' And so he did."

In a sense, we can say that God said the same thing to *(name)*. God said, "*(Name)*, you look very tired. Why don't you come to My place and stay and rest?"

And that poetic way of looking at *(name's)* departure from our presence may comfort us. But we do not say that God caused *(name's)* death. People may say, "God called him home," or, "God took him," but God did not create death nor does He cause it.

Death comes upon us because of our sinful condition. We—all of us—are mortal, meaning that one day we, too, will die. Why? We inherited our sinful, mortal condition from the parents of the human race, Adam and Eve.

In addition to inheriting Adam's mortality, the result of original sin, we also are guilty of our own sin. In our sins of commission and omission, we have placed ourselves first, ahead of God and others, whom we assign a lower priority. Sin is just that: self-absorption and self-centeredness. Sin is ignoring God and planning our lives as if He did not exist.

We Christians have been redeemed by God in Christ Jesus. Our sins are forgiven—the sin passed down to us from Adam, as well as the sins we ourselves commit. All are wiped clean by our Lord Jesus Christ, who suffered on the cross for the sins of all people. Jesus died. Death came to Him as a member of the human race, though He was without sin. His resurrection from the grave is our comfort and our hope in all aspects of our Christian life and especially at this time.

A funeral like this is a sober reminder of what is truly important in life. Christ's Church on earth—fallible as we all admit the Church is as an institution—is our place of birth as Christians, and it is where we are finally laid to rest. Our spiritual birth—actually, our rebirth—took place in Holy Baptism. Our sins were forgiven by the gracious, redemptive power of God through the resurrection of Christ Jesus (1 Pet 3:21). The Holy Spirit descended upon us to fill us with new life. And throughout our earthly existence that new life is nourished in worship by the Word of God and Holy Communion, where we receive Christ's body and blood, given and shed for the forgiveness of our sin. The liturgy of the Church, so full of rich insights, teaches us the truths of God and puts songs of faith in our hearts. All this prepares us for the final time when the sign of the cross is made over us and we are laid to rest in the confident hope of the resurrection of the dead.

God is not a God of "cheap grace," easy forgiveness. The payment for our sins cost Him the life of His Son—our Savior. But by Christ's death and resurrection, we are forgiven people. God declares us righteous—made right again in His eyes— through Christ's atoning work for us. We cannot save ourselves. Christ did save us. And He wants the assurance and peace and comfort and hope of that forgiveness to be a living reality in our daily lives. God says: "Behold, I have engraved you on the palms of My hands" (Is 49:16). "I have redeemed you . . . you are Mine" (Is 43:1).

(Name) believed that. He was baptized and knew he was a forgiven child of God. He read a lot, including Koehler's *Summary of Christian Doctrine* (or insert similar example). *(Name)* and I talked about that book and another book he was intensely interested in about the nature of Christ. I said I would get a copy of another book for him, and he was looking forward to receiving it. Because of his illness, I was not able to put it into his hands. It was titled *Life with God*. And that's what *(name)* has right now: life with God. Three words sum up *(name's)* state right now. These three words are "with the Lord." That's what life eternal is: being in the presence of the eternal God who is love. That is joyful bliss beyond all description.

We here today are human, and we sorrow at losing *(name)*. But *(name)* would not have us grieve, for he is "with the Lord"! Just imagine for a moment what *(name)* would say to us if he could speak to us now. If he were to write us a letter, it might sound like this:

A final letter to my wife, *(name)*, my children, *(names)*, and all who have known me: I may have suffered during my earthly life, but all is different now. I am beyond any pain, any discomfort. By God's grace in His Son, Jesus Christ, I now am in the presence of God. You are the ones in pain. But in heaven, you, too, will not know pain. So if you hurt, I am truly sorry. But dwell on the joys— the many joyful times God permitted us to have together.

Remember our common faith in our Lord and Savior, Jesus Christ. That faith you confess in the Creed is the same faith held dear by us in heaven too.

I love each of you so much—each in a special and different way. So now rejoice! Christ died for us and rose again! And because of that, I will see you again!

Rev. Donald L. Deffner

A Soldier's Faith

Matthew 8:5–13

(Name) was a soldier. He took great pride in the fact that he served our nation with distinction and honor. As we gather in this place today, we come to give honor and praise to God for the blessings He extended to *(name)* during his earthly life. Among those blessings were his dedication to his wife and family, his commitment to his church and country, and his concern for those whom he knew.

As I prepared for this service today, I gave thought to *(name's)* military career and the rank he achieved over time. Like a good soldier, *(name)* knew what it was like to take orders as well as what it was like to give them. He was dedicated to those above him and devoted to those under his command. As I gave thought to these things, I was reminded of a story of another soldier who had a conversation with our Lord Jesus Christ. That event is found in Mt 8:5–13.

What I want to talk to you about today is a soldier's faith.

FAITH REALIZES ITS UNWORTHINESS

The soldier in our text was a centurion, a Roman soldier in charge of a garrison of one hundred men. Therefore, he knew how to give orders and how to take them. We are told that he had a servant who was quite ill. The centurion came to Jesus and asked Him to heal his servant. Jesus responded by saying, "I will come and heal him" (v. 7). It is the dialogue that follows that is so interesting.

"The centurion replied [to Jesus], 'Lord, I am not worthy to have You come under my roof' " (v. 8). We are not quite sure why the soldier said that. Whatever the reason, the soldier realized that the healing he sought was neither earned nor deserved.

In the same way, we, too, are not worthy of God's grace and mercy. He does not answer our prayers or receive us into His kingdom because we have achieved some great honor, attained a great rank, or completed a great task. The hymn writer said it best when he wrote in the great hymn "Rock of Ages": "Nothing in my hand I bring; Simply to Thy cross I cling" (*LSB* 761:3).

FAITH ACKNOWLEDGES THE POWER
AND AUTHORITY OF CHRIST

The centurion said, "Only say the word, and my servant will be healed. For I too am a man under authority, with soldiers under me. And I say to one, 'Go,' and he goes, and to another, 'Come,' and he comes, and to my servant, 'Do this,' and he does it" (vv. 8–9).

What the centurion recognizes is that Christ is a person who has authority—not just any authority, but a divine authority, the authority of God Himself. Christ has the authority to forgive sins, to order and direct our lives in relationship with Him. His authority comes not just from His being God but by virtue of His victory in the battle against sin, death, and the devil. This soldier, Jesus Christ, fought in our place, died in our place, and rose—*Christus Victor*, Christ the Victor!

We human beings often resist authority. From the time we are very young we want to establish our own independence and control our own lives. Often we may resist God's authority. We fear that somehow we may lose our freedom. Nothing could be further from the truth. God desires to have authority not to dictate over us but to deliver us from things that would enslave us.

We carry many heavy burdens in the course of our life. Many times we carry a burden of guilt over things we have said or done, or a burden of grief because we did not say or do other things. Today I proclaim to you the Good News that the same Lord who brought healing to the soldier's servant can bring comfort and relief to you as well. Today Christ's authority over death assures you of *(name's)* eternal life!

Faith Trusts the Word

The soldier said, "Only say the word." That's faith. That's trust. Our text tells us that Jesus was astonished at the man's faith. The faith the soldier exhibited is the faith we are called to have as well. Whether that faith trusts in God's provision for our daily needs or clings to God's promises of a home in heaven in the last hours of earthly life is of little moment. We can trust the Word of God because of the authority given to Christ Jesus.

As *(name's)* pastor, I had an opportunity to get to know him. What stands out in my mind are a couple of war stories he told me. He told me how frightened he was on D-Day when he was about to land on Normandy Beach in France. Yet he did not focus on his fear but on how he shared his faith with another soldier who was equally frightened. He told me how his faith in Christ gave him hope for release when he became a prisoner of war. Indeed, these two episodes spoke of trusting the Word of Christ in very desperate situations. In our daily struggles, we, too, can trust the Word of Christ. He has not only delivered us from trials in the past, but He also will keep us safe in times that lie ahead.

As the centurion would say to his servant, "Come," and he comes, so our heavenly Father said to *(name)*, "Come, and inherit the place I have prepared for you." *(Name)*, as a good soldier, heard the order and departed this earthly life to be with his Lord and Savior for all eternity. For this great gift we say, Thanks be to God.

Rev. Samuel E. McPeek

He Breathed His Last

Luke 23:44–49

The reading for this morning highlights the depth of the connection between our brother in Christ, *(name)*, and our Lord. That connection is what this service and his life are about. What is remarkable here is not that *(name)* died, but that he died so well. Listen to these words from St. Luke's Gospel concerning Jesus on the cross:

> It was now about the sixth hour, and there was darkness over the whole land until the ninth hour, while the sun's light failed. And the curtain of the temple was torn in two. Then Jesus, calling out with a loud voice, said, "Father, into Your hands I commit My spirit!" And having said this He breathed His last. Now when the centurion saw what had taken place, he praised God, saying, "Certainly this man was innocent!" And all the crowds that had assembled for this spectacle, when they saw what had taken place, returned home beating their breasts. And all His acquaintances and the women who had followed Him from Galilee stood at a distance watching these things. (Lk 23:44–49)

Most of us here know that *(name)* fought with emphysema for a long time. Lately, the struggle to breathe had not gone well, so he had been in and out of the hospital. One of the things that commends this passage from Luke are these words: "He breathed His last." Our Lord knew what it was to labor for each small catch of air and then, finally, to lose. One of the tortures of crucifixion was the possibility of dying from asphyxiation before bleeding to death or dying of shock. Jesus knew and endured the suffering *(name)* knew and endured.

But why talk about Jesus' death? Why focus on someone else when we should be thinking about *(name)*? Because *(name)* and Jesus shared in death what they shared in life and what they now share in eternity. Jesus' death was *(name's)* death and *(name's)* death was Jesus' death. They shared in the same story—lived a single life between them.

He Confessed the Faith

This sounds odd to our ears, but let's think about it for a moment. *(Name)* and Jesus were bound together in Word and Sacrament. At the altar *(name)* was given Jesus' flesh and blood to eat and drink for the forgiveness of his sins. He came faithfully to hear the Gospel proclaimed, the Gospel that repeatedly assured him that Jesus is the vine and we are the branches, that we are one with Him even as He and the Father are one. At the font *(name)* was baptized into both the death

28

and the resurrection of Jesus Christ. They had one body, that of Jesus Christ, and they had one Spirit, God the Holy Spirit.

So how do we know this is true? How do we know that *(name)* and Jesus were so intimately bound together? We know this because of the good confession *(name)* made. He witnessed to the faith and stood up to be counted among the people of God. He confessed the faith in the language of the Church from ancient times. He spoke the creeds in the company of his fellow Christians and sang the hymns of the Church.

But there was another way, a very important way, in which *(name)* confessed the faith. He lived according to the Word of God and let the light of Christ shine through him into the lives of others. *(Name)* confessed the faith, the truth that he and his Lord were one, because Christ lived in him and everyone could see that.

He Lived the Faith

(Name) confessed the faith by being a good father. His children wanted everyone to know how good a father *(name)* was, but it hardly needs to be said. It can be seen by the love they have for him. A Christian father is one who patterns his care after the care God shows us. *(Name)* was that kind of parent. When his children were in need or merely wanted something, even something as inconsequential as a chocolate shake, he would get it for them if it was good for them—not if it was convenient for him, but if it was good for them.

Being a Christian father goes hand in hand with being a Christian husband. *(Name)* was both. He confessed the faith in his love and devotion to *(name)*. To be a good husband is to love your wife as Christ loves His Church. *(Name)* and his wife never wanted to be apart if they didn't absolutely have to be. By insisting that they not be apart, he was confessing that God had put them together.

He took in stride service in the infantry during World War II, a burden borne by so many of his generation. I can't say he was unmarked by that service, but he was certainly not destroyed by it. It did not diminish him. He was a soldier, an infantryman, a man of arms, yet right up to the end, he was always gentle. It was not his sinful human nature that made him so peaceful. It was the life of Christ within him, which he confessed quietly.

He Waited on God

He also confessed the faith by being loyal, devoted, and patient. Forty-nine years of Christian marriage and thirty-seven years at his job are proof that he was content and able to wait on the Lord. It was significant to him that he had lived in Kansas for twenty years, even though he had been away from there longer than he had lived there. He was content to live according to God's time.

29

Of the daily confessions *(name)* made throughout his life, I am most familiar with his genuine concern for his fellow man. During the long weeks in the hospital, he got to know the nurses and their families—how many children they have, where they were born—and voiced his Christian love for them.

Seven or eight weeks ago, when *(name)* went to the emergency room and then to intensive care, he felt he had been close to death. He described something like tunnel vision, but more important, he was absolutely certain that he had felt the presence of Jesus. Some might ask, "How could he feel Jesus with him?" A far better question is, "How could he not?" As closely bound to Christ as this Christian was, it is not at all surprising that when death seemed imminent his Lord would be present. *(Name's)* unshakable conviction that Jesus died for his sins and thus united him to his heavenly Father was God's greatest gift to our friend. It was that confidence in the forgiving grace of Jesus that made *(name's)* life what it was and is.

How terrible might those moments in the emergency room have been had he not had that faith? How dreadful would it be to face death without the rock solid assurance that Christ will face it with you and that you are guaranteed victory in him? What misery it would be not to know what would come after death, only to find that it was the unspeakable loneliness of hell! *(Name)* had no such fears, and his courage in the face of death was a beautiful confession of God's grace.

The faith that *(name)* confessed so simply yet so fully, his genuine bond with Jesus, is the same faith God our Father has given us. What sustained *(name)* throughout life and through the gates of death will sustain us as we wait to follow him in God's good time. We look forward to the resurrection with the same confidence we saw in *(name)*. What was true for *(name)* is also true for us.

(Name's) life is like Jesus' life. On the cross, Jesus breathed His last breath, but on Easter His breath was back. On *(date)*, *(name)* breathed his last breath, but now he has his breath back. Although his death may leave us breathless for a while, by God's grace we, too, will have our breath restored in God's good time.

Rev. Charles E. Varsogea

Question Marks Turned into Exclamation Points

Luke 24:1–8

The Christian faith is a life of paradox. My dictionary notes a paradox is "a statement that is seemingly contradictory or opposed to common sense and yet is perhaps true."[1] It is two words or thoughts that don't seem to go together. For example, "The last will be first, and the first last" (Mt 20:16) and "Whoever would be great among you must be your servant, and whoever would be first among you must be your slave" (Mt 20:26–27). Some other examples: In weakness there is strength. In grief there is hope. In tragedy there is triumph. We are at the same time both sinner and saint. And the most astounding paradox: in death there is life.

Your tears and emotions today are also a paradox. One moment they might be tears of grief, the next, tears of joy and laughter. Today may also be a day of questions. "Why, Lord? Why this family?" "What's the purpose in this, Lord? What good could possibly come from this?" "Why didn't You heal her?" "What will happen to her family? her two children?"

As *(name)* struggled with her cancer, I have to confess that I struggled with her Creator. In my pain I penned these words:

Can you heal, Lord? I believe You can!

But will You heal, Lord? I'll leave that in Your hand.

Cancer, Lord. That's what the doctor diagnosed today.

This piranha-like disease eats not only flesh, but families and faith away.

They sent her home saying, "Sorry, there's nothing we can do."

And so, I realize; her only hope is You.

Can You heal, Lord? I believe You can!

But will You heal, Lord? I'll leave that in Your hand.

The comfort I have found is that God desires to take the question marks of my life, sparked by fear, and replace them with exclamation points of praise, ignited by faith. He wants to replace my doubt with faith.

---

1   *Merriam-Webster's Collegiate Dictionary*, 11th ed. (Springfield, MA: Merriam-Webster, 2003).

Our text, Lk 24:1–8, is an example of how God takes question marks, straightens them out, and turns them into exclamation points. The women who went to anoint the body of the Lord that first Easter morning went to the tomb filled with grief. With tears of pain in their hearts, they found, to their surprise, that the stone had been rolled away. The angel said to them, "Why do you seek the living among the dead?" (Lk 24:5).

The problem those women faced on that first Easter morning and that you and I face today is that our pain causes us to focus on the question marks of fear instead of on the exclamation points of promise. Our pain at the death of (name) causes us to forget the promise of the resurrection. Our pain at the separation causes us to forget the promise of a reunion.

The text continues, "They remembered His words" (Lk 24:8). Jesus had said after He had been crucified by sinful men, He would "on the third day rise" (Lk 24:7). The women remember His promise. With great joy and excitement, they run to tell the others: "He's alive! The tomb is empty! It's just like He said!"

Remember! Rejoice!

With God's help, we should do two things today. First, we should remember. Remember the God-given, God-guided, God-graced life of *(name)*. Remember, through our pain, the promise of the resurrection. Remember the death and resurrection of Christ for the sins of humanity so we have not just life, but eternal life. Only if we remember God's salvation promise can we accomplish the second thing.

Second, we should rejoice. Rejoice and celebrate the life of a woman who touched so many lives. Rejoice and celebrate the life, death, and resurrection of her Savior who touched her life in such a dramatic fashion. So let's do both today. Let's remember and let's rejoice. Let's ask God to replace the questions marks caused by our pain with exclamation points of praise. As we remember and rejoice in the life of *(name)*, let me divide her life into four stages. Each stage centers around the person of Jesus Christ.

First Stage: Life without Christ

(Name) began life on *(date)*, born, as we all are, with a terminal spiritual disease. Because of our nature, sin and death hound us. The moment we are born is the moment we begin to die. Because of our inherited sin, we are all terminally ill.

The apostle Paul describes our life with these words: "And you were dead in the trespasses and sins" (Eph 2:1), and "You were at that time separated from Christ . . . having no hope and without God in the world" (Eph 2:12). This is the condition of anyone who is without faith in Christ Jesus. *(Name)* understood this terminal condition. This was the first stage of her life: born into this world without Christ.

This first stage didn't last long. Her parents brought her to the waters of Baptism on *(date)*, at *(name of church where baptized)*, and by the grace of God she experienced a second birth—a spiritual birth into the family of God. Her sins were washed away. She was connected to the death and the resurrection of Jesus Christ. She became a new creation—a child of God. At her Baptism she was no longer without Christ. She entered the second stage of her life—a life in Christ. She had been "crucified with Christ. It is no longer [she] who [lived], but Christ who [lived in her]" (Gal 2:20).

SECOND STAGE: LIFE IN CHRIST JESUS

Throughout her adolescence, she grew in faith and knowledge of the Savior. At *(name of church where she was confirmed)*, from *(name of pastor)*, *(name)* learned about the triune God in the Apostles' Creed; the will of God in the Ten Commandments; how to pray using the Lord's Prayer; the grace and forgiveness of God given in the Sacraments and in the Office of the Keys. She was no longer without Christ but in Christ. As the apostle Paul says, "But now in Christ Jesus you who once were far off have been brought near by the blood of Christ" (Eph 2:13). By the Spirit's work she was connected to Christ Jesus and was being transformed into His likeness. Being in Christ led to the third stage of her life—a life lived for Christ.

THIRD STAGE: LIFE LIVED FOR CHRIST

I shared this verse many times with *(name)*. "For to me to live is Christ, and to die is gain" (Phil 1:21). In talking with you, the family and friends of *(name)*, memory after memory surfaced that reflected her Christlike character—her Christlike life. *(Insert personal moments and/or comments shared by the family.)*

Throughout her life, *(name)* pointed to the cross of Jesus Christ. She pointed to His grace, His forgiveness, His faithfulness. *(Name's)* words to you today would be, "I have not abandoned you but rather I have gone ahead of you." This leads to the fourth and final stage of her life—a life forever with Christ Jesus in paradise!

FOURTH STAGE: LIFE WITH CHRIST

This stage is cause for rejoicing. The apostle John paints such a beautiful picture of the life that *(name)* now enjoys. "After this I looked, and behold, a great multitude that no one could number, from every nation, from all tribes and peoples and languages, standing before the throne and before the Lamb, clothed in white robes, with palm branches in their hands" (Rev 7:9).

This multitude of saints cries out and sings eternal praises to the Lamb who is seated on the throne. Then the apostle describes the eternal life these saints enjoy:

> Therefore they are before the throne of God, and serve Him day and night in His temple; and He who sits on the throne will shelter them with His presence. They shall hunger no more, neither thirst anymore; the sun shall not strike them, nor any scorching heat. For the Lamb in the midst of the throne will be their shepherd, and He will guide them to springs of living water, and God will wipe away every tear from their eyes. (Rev 7:15–17)

(Name) is in the presence of the Savior, worshiping with the angels. The Good News is that one day we, too, who were once without Christ, who by grace through faith are now in Christ, and who by grace live for Christ, will also, by grace, one day be with Christ and with *(name)*.

When that day comes, we won't remember the questions we asked God this past year. But we will do these two things: We will remember and we will rejoice. We will remember the grace of God upon our life—His faithfulness and His compassion and His loving touch. And we will rejoice with exclamation points of praise. In the pain of today and the days to come, may God help you to remember the promise of the resurrection.

Why do you look for the living among the dead (question mark)? He is not here! He has risen (exclamation point)!

Rev. Paul W. Arndt

Completing the Picture

1 Corinthians 13:12b

Helen enjoyed putting together difficult jigsaw puzzles. The thousand-piece variety was the kind she enjoyed most because it challenged her concentration, her perseverance, and her desire to get the puzzle completed. During my regular visits with Helen, I would offer to put at least one piece in place in the mammoth puzzle. Oftentimes, however, I would confess to her that my perseverance for putting that one piece in its proper place was not always great. I told her how easy it would be for me to throw up my hands in despair and say, "That's too tough for me!" Helen admitted that she sometimes felt the puzzle was a greater match for her than she could handle. How frustrating it can be, for instance, to be so close to completing the puzzle and yet be so burdened by those final pieces waiting to be put in place. But without those final pieces the picture is incomplete.

I shared with Helen that such a challenge for completing that picture puzzle is a microcosm of her life. Over the past two years when she faced the ill effects of disease she would from time to time be frustrated that the final pieces of her life's picture were not being put in place very well. When it comes to our life as God's children we don't see the complete picture on this side of the grave. Our physical eyes and our minds aren't able to grasp the full panoramic view. The doctors informed Helen and you members of her family, "We cannot pinpoint how the disease started. But we will treat it as best as we can. There are no guarantees regarding the treatment of this disease. It's all in God's hands."

We saw the effects of the disease and the strain it put on family and friends. But we also know the gift God has bestowed upon us through His Son, Jesus Christ. It is Jesus' presence that serves as the setting for God's love enfolding us. This day as we lay the mortal remains of your loved one and our dear sister in the faith in their final resting place, we do so with the confidence that the apostle Peter expressed to Jesus, "Lord, to whom shall we go? You have the words of eternal life, and we have believed, and have come to know, that You are the Holy One of God" (Jn 6:68–69). It is Jesus who completes the picture for the life of the child of God.

THE PICTURE FOR OUR LIVES IS COMPLETE IN ETERNITY

The apostle Paul writes in 1 Corinthians, "Now I know in part" (13:12). The picture for our life is not complete in this life. It is complete on the other side of the grave in eternal life. We wonder what heaven will be like. We know in part through what God tells us in His Word: the absence of pain, suffering, and disease; no tears, sorrow, or death. The absence of those negatives affirms that sin is not in the picture when it comes to eternal life in heaven.

The child of God knows why he dies. Helen knew why she would die. She realized that she was connected to our first parents, Adam and Eve. Their fall into sin meant that she also was a sinner; likewise, we all are. For her to receive eternal life would come not because of the blessing she was to you, her loved ones, or to her brothers and sisters in Christ in this congregation, or to her community. It is Jesus' death on the cross and resurrection from the grave that paid the price for Helen's sins, your sins, and my sins. By God's gift of faith, which Helen received in the washing of Holy Baptism, the Holy Spirit connected the benefits of Jesus' death and resurrection to her. It is by God's Holy Word and the Sacrament of the Lord's Supper that the Holy Spirit nurtured that saving faith in her heart so that though she wouldn't know what the completed picture was for her, she knew the one who did know—her Savior from sin to everlasting life—Jesus Christ.

What Heaven Will Be Like

"I wonder what heaven will be like." The Scriptures show us that not only will there be the absence of the negatives but also the presence of lasting peace and joy, the beauty of being with Jesus. As Jesus said to the repentant thief on the cross, "Truly, I say to you, today you will be with Me in Paradise" (Lk 23:43), so He says to each person who dies in faith.

St. Paul adds in that same verse in 1 Corinthians 13, "Then I shall know fully" (v. 12). God will reveal the complete picture for us when He calls us to our heavenly home. Helen's sufferings were great, especially in her last two years of life on this earth. Yet how much greater is the joy of dwelling in God's presence eternally. Then all of the suffering we may experience on this earth shall be as a "drop in the bucket" compared to the joy of being with Jesus. We will be wrapped up in the power and peace of Jesus' presence. That is the confident certainty we have by grace through our faith in Jesus Christ. He will complete the picture for us when He calls us to our heavenly home. Then we will know fully the joy of eternal life with Jesus.

We Are Fully Known by Jesus

"Now I know in part; then I shall know fully, even as I have been fully known" (1 Cor 13:12). The tentacles of our sinful nature create the frustration of not having the picture complete on this side of the grave. We wish we knew fully now what we will know fully in heaven. But we are fully known by our Lord Jesus Christ, who has gone through death's door and risen victoriously from the grave for us. We take comfort in that. The Lord who made us knows our needs. He knows the concerns that are deep within the crevices of our hearts. He knows the frustrations we feel when our life is faced with the roller-coaster existence of good days and bad days, days of joy and days of mourning.

Helen was fully known by her Lord and Savior, Jesus Christ. In her prayers she could pour out her frustrations to her Lord and know that her Savior's shoulders were big enough to handle her frustrations, her Savior's heart was big enough to receive them, her Savior's Word was powerful enough to convey the good news of His divine love for her—His child and heir of eternal life.

You, dear loved ones, are also known by our Lord Jesus Christ. He knows your times of grief and sorrow. He knows your weaknesses. He knows your needs. By His Word and Sacrament He blesses all of us with His presence, which gives us forgiveness, life, encouragement, and guidance. By His Word of promise through His means of grace He accompanies us in our journey through the valleys of the shadows of death when the picture of our life, like a puzzle, is incomplete for our eyes to behold. By His Word of promise through His means of grace we are fully known so that we can know He will complete the picture for us. The risen Lord Jesus is your guarantee. You have His Word on it!

Rev. Kenneth J. Gerike

God's Grace Goes with Us

1 Corinthians 15:10

At a time of grieving like this, those who are here present, and I on behalf of this congregation, offer your family and all who were closest to the departed our deepest sympathy. May our dear Lord, who knows your needs, comfort you, and give you strength and faith to uphold one another.

Whenever people gather for a Christian funeral, there are two basic reasons for the worship service: (1) to demonstrate by our presence the respect we have for the deceased, a life given as a trust from God, and (2) to contemplate the meaning of our relationship to God and to other people for time and eternity.

For this consideration, our text is most appropriate, for it takes note of individuality and relates life to the grace of God. There is no more meaningful or beautiful concept for human beings to contemplate than the grace of God. It emphasizes that God is not only great but also good. Our life on earth is uncertain and precarious. We see the grace of God not only in how He sustains us by every breath we draw but also in the knowledge that we are in His hands and accountable to Him. The grace of God is always undeserved love and care. As a family you have experienced the grace of God in many ways, not least of all in one another. But God's grace is evident most clearly in how God has restored our relationship to Himself, a relationship that was broken by human sin.

We know that grace clearly in the Bible statement so often repeated among Christians, Jn 3:16. In that verse, which some of you have surely committed to memory, we read, "For God so loved the world, that He gave His only Son, that whoever believes in Him should not perish but have eternal life." Whether we celebrate birth or marriage, whether we experience success or failure, whether we struggle with illness or rejoice in our health, whether we gather as families to feast at Thanksgiving or to mourn at a funeral, we find life's fullest and final meaning always in the grace of God.

The apostle Paul, who wrote the words of our text to the Corinthian Christians, bears testimony to the significance of God's grace. Paul had experienced God's grace powerfully in coming to faith. Do you remember how Jesus touched Paul's life when he was on the road to Damascus as an enemy and persecutor of Christians? By that experience, and the instruction and Baptism that followed it, Paul's life was turned in a new direction. Instead of hunting Christians to persecute, he traveled endlessly to bring the message of salvation to distant people.

Paul attributes to God's grace the change in his life and his witness to Christ. Paul declares, "By the grace of God I am what I am." So for us and for all Christians, our Baptism and hearing of the Gospel, our daily strength and blessings, and our hope of heaven are all properly recognized as coming from God's grace.

It is only fitting that we should today gratefully testify that God's grace was also the greatest thing in the life of the departed. There are many things to be grateful for: years of life, family, work, special interests, and achievements. All of these stem from the gift of God that Paul calls grace. Of the departed it was also true: "By the grace of God I am what I am." The departed recognized God's grace as witnessed by church attendance and the actions and attitudes of life. For all who believe, even one's own weaknesses and sins are overcome by God's grace in Christ.

The grace of God did not come to the departed in vain, as Paul says. Unfortunately and sadly, many who are dependent on the grace of God—as we all are, even for life itself—do not give God thanks or glory for His grace. Now, at the end of this life that we lay to rest today, because God's grace was sought, was received, and was trusted, you can be comforted by the promise of eternal life in the presence of God Himself.

The amount of comfort and hope given by the grace of God is never more clearly evident than when a Christian's life comes to an end on earth. The entire chapter of 1 Corinthians 15 is an account by Paul of the hope and assurance we have because of God's grace in Christ. Paul rests all evidence of our eternal hope on the resurrection of Jesus Christ from the dead. Jesus, who died on the cross for our sins, rose again to assure us that the victory is won.

No one can claim to stand blameless before God by his own merit. Neither do we claim that for the departed. But we firmly believe, as God's Word tells us, that "the blood of Jesus [God's] Son cleanses us from all sin" (1 Jn 1:7). It is this confidence in the grace of God that brings peace and comfort to you now. That confidence will help you even more than the good memories you hold—and it is wise to share those memories with one another at this time. But the grace of God will sustain you, as it did the departed.

At the end of 1 Corinthians 15, the apostle Paul writes words that give a fitting exhortation to you as you go forward in God's grace: "Therefore, my beloved brothers, be steadfast, immovable, always abounding in the work of the Lord, knowing that in the Lord your labor is not in vain" (1 Cor 15:58).

Rev. Omar Stuenkel

But in Fact . . .

1 Corinthians 15:12–26

We are here because *(name)* died. His death was untimely, and the news caught most of us by surprise. Without warning, his family and friends face the loss of *(name)* from their midst. Now we are here together. Each of us bears a sadness. Each of us feels an emptiness that comes when someone near and dear to us is suddenly gone. While some may seek comfort in the hope that time heals all wounds, as Christians we turn to the Word of God, where we find comfort and joy as God's people.

Is Death Final?

Can this body, which once enjoyed youth and vigor, ever really die? *(Name's)* body was reliable for many years, generally in good health and suffering illness only occasionally. *(Name's)* children grew up with a strong father, whose body was able to earn a living, play ball, work on science fair projects, and romp with his grandchildren. When *(name's)* body grew weaker with age, it seemed only a minor problem. In our minds we still saw *(name)* as an active, vibrant individual with much life in him. When he suffered a heart attack, it was with shock and then disbelief that we saw him on life-support systems. At first we denied death could happen, and then we felt helpless when it seemed inevitable.

How do we handle the possibility of death? Some people believe we can overcome its intrusion—surely the medical advancements of today postpone death—but every medical doctor admits that 100 percent of their patients eventually die. Others believe life is a matter of sheer will. Still others ignore the possibility of death or shrug their shoulders and say, "It's fate." No human answer is satisfactory.

In Christ All Will Be Made Alive

In our text, St. Paul wrote to the Corinthian Christians, who grew up disbelieving in the physical resurrection of the dead. For them, death was the final statement in any person's life. Paul responded with the Good News of the Gospel. First, that God's Son took the sins of the world upon Himself and died to pay that terrible debt. But death was not the last word in Jesus' life. Second, God raised Jesus from the dead as acknowledgment of His Son's payment. Because Jesus was raised, His death for our sins was accepted. Jesus was raised for our justification, that is, we are made right with God through Jesus' payment.

Paul is not proclaiming myths or fables, but truth. Our faith, which hears these words and accepts them, is not useless; it holds solid comfort. We are not still in our sins, stuck in the dead-end direction of damnation. Those who die in the hope of their Lord are not lost. They live in Him.

Christianity is not some gimmick to get us through this present life. It is not some ethical system to help us deal with present realities. Christianity is the confession of the crucified and risen Lord, who brings life from death.

(Name) clung to the promises found in God's Word. It was God's Word that called *(name)* to receive the gift of life in the promises of his Baptism. He confirmed his belief in Christ as a young man. He bore witness to his faith in Christ by worshiping the Lord. He heard and responded to the promise our Lord made in His Last Supper, "Given and shed for you for the forgiveness of sins." Jesus was the living bread in *(name's)* life, and in Jesus *(name)* knew he had eternal life (Jn 6:51). God worked grace in *(name's)* life through the Word, and by the power of the Spirit *(name)* received the gift of life in Jesus' name. *(Name)* believed his sins were fully paid for on the cross and that his dear Lord won for him eternal life by grace through faith. This was *(name's)* witness, what he believed. And this was his hope that he shared with his family and friends.

God's Comfort

How do we feel? Are we sad? Yes. Do we feel an emptiness where *(name)* touched our lives? Yes. Do we feel hopeless? No! In Jesus' words we find hope and life, which fill us with assurance from the One who rose from the dead and is the Author of hope for us.

Our resurrected Lord, the Lord of life, the one who conquered death for us, said, "Be faithful unto death, and I will give you the crown of life" (Rev 2:10). There is nothing more comforting for those who are sad and miss a loved one than to find strength in these words. Our hope is in the Lord, and our comfort is to know that those who are faithful in Jesus will live together and rejoice together for eternal life. When we come to worship and join in the Divine Service with our hymns of praise and come to the Communion table to receive Christ's body and blood, we join with all of heaven in the joy of the resurrection. We are never nearer to those "who in glory shine" than when we are with our Lord. We recall the stirring words of victory in the Communion liturgy, "With angels and archangels and with all the company of heaven we laud and magnify Your glorious name evermore praising You and saying . . ." (*Lutheran Service Book: Altar Book*, p. 161).

We are here because *(name)* died, and we need to receive the hopeful words our dear Lord gives us. May His words of life, given through His death and resurrection, be our source of comfort and assurance.

Rev. Eric C. Stumpf

41

Grieving with Hope

1 Thessalonians 4:13–18

Andrew

Funerals and grief go together. Sadness and bereavement are normal when a loved one dies; but there is a significant difference in the type of grief evidenced at funerals.

On the one hand, there are many funerals where the sorrow of the bereaved is inconsolable, where widows or widowers and children of the deceased weep and lament without hope. Nothing anyone says or does can allay their grief. On the other hand, at Christian funerals and memorial services, the bereaved also evidence great sadness, but mixed with their sadness is their Christian hope, which enables them to dry their tears and even smile in the midst of their sorrow.

St. Paul speaks of this significant difference in grieving when he writes in the words of our text, "We do not want you to be uninformed, brothers, about those who are asleep, that you may not grieve as others do who have no hope" (v. 13). The apostle goes on to say that believers in Christ, by contrast, grieve with hope! This hope is expressed in the closing words of the Apostles' Creed: "I believe in . . . the resurrection of the body, and the life everlasting. Amen."

WE GRIEVE WITH HOPE
BECAUSE WE DO NOT HAVE TO FEAR DEATH

There is probably nothing in life that people fear more than death. This fear is demonstrated in the fact that we avoid the noun *death* and the verb *die*. In medical circles, a patient doesn't die; instead, he or she "expires." In daily conversation, we often employ the euphemism "passed away" rather than say that a person has died.

We who are believers in Christ do not have to be afraid of death. Jesus explained why we need not fear death when He said to Martha, "I am the resurrection and the life. Whoever believes in Me, though he die, yet shall he live, and everyone who lives and believes in Me shall never die" (Jn 11:25–26). For those who trust in Jesus for forgiveness and life, death is but the door through which they enter into an even better life. By His death and triumphant resurrection, Jesus has made complete payment for all sins.

It's interesting that St. Paul refers to death three times in our text as a "sleep." Paul writes about "the dead in Christ" (v. 16): "We do not want you to be uninformed, brothers, about those who are asleep. . . . God will bring with Him those who have fallen asleep. . . . We who are alive . . . will not precede those who have fallen asleep" (vv. 13–15).

It's a pleasant experience to fall asleep, especially if we are tired after a day of hard work. Actually, the bad experience is to be unable to sleep, to toss and turn as we wait for morning to come. To sleep is pleasant, and to awaken from sleep refreshed and strengthened is one of the most pleasant experiences of all.

When St. Paul refers to death as a sleep, he is saying in a very powerful way that you and I who believe in Jesus do not have to be afraid of death any more than we are afraid of falling asleep at the end of the day. That's why our parents taught us at an early age to pray at bedtime: "Now I lay me down to sleep. I pray the Lord my soul to keep; and if I die before I wake, I pray the Lord my soul to take; and this I ask for Jesus' sake."

We Grieve with Hope
because We Can Look forward to Eternal Life

We who believe in Jesus Christ do not grieve without hope and do not fear death, because our faith in Christ assures us of the gift of eternal life. Jesus Himself said this in the best-known Bible verse of all when He declared, "For God so loved the world, that He gave His only Son, that whoever believes in Him should not perish but have eternal life" (Jn 3:16).

It was more than thirty-five years ago, but I'll never forget what my wife said to me as we were leaving the church after my father's funeral service. Squeezing my arm, she whispered, "Honey, how can anyone who doesn't believe in Jesus cope with the death of a loved one?" How true! To be separated by death from a loved one is a frightening experience. But we know that death for the child of God is the beginning of an even better life, and we look forward to a joyful reunion in heaven.

St. Paul speaks of that day of celebration when he writes in our text: "The Lord Himself will descend from heaven with a cry of command, with the voice of an archangel, and with the sound of the trumpet of God. And the dead in Christ will rise first. Then we who are alive, who are left, will be caught up together with them in the clouds to meet the Lord in the air, and so we will always be with the Lord" (vv. 16–17).

"And so we will always be with the Lord"! We can't really imagine or comprehend what eternal life will be like.

One Sunday School youngster did a pretty good job of summarizing the joy of eternal life when she was asked to define heaven. "Heaven," said the little girl, "is when it's Christmas every day!" What a precious and accurate summary! We all remember the days of our childhood, when we couldn't wait for Christmas to come. And when that great day finally arrived, we wished that the joy of Christmas would last forever.

And it will! That's why the apostle concludes by saying, "Therefore encourage one another with these words" (v. 18).

Rev. Oscar A. Gerken

A Burden to Bear, a Hope to Share, a Lord to Care

1 Thessalonians 4:13–18

In Christ, our risen and present Lord, dear *(name close family members)*:

Every life has two portals. One is birth, and the other is death, so the wisdom writer affirms, "For everything there is a season, and a time for every matter under heaven: a time to be born, and a time to die" (Eccl 3:1–2). Death has come knocking at your door. Death—the most brutal enemy of life, an unwelcome intruder in your family fellowship. *(Name)* will not be part of our lives until God's kingdom comes in glory. In the language of hope, she is forever with the Lord.

In times of sorrow our feelings run amok. They need tempering, and Christ alone can provide the right prescription. There is a verse of consolation in Scripture: "Precious in the sight of the Lord is the death of His saints" (Ps 116:15). Together with our primary reading from 1 Thessalonians, I offer you three words of consolation—three divine truths, if you will—for the comfort your spirits are yearning. I pray that these words will give fuel to the fire of your faith in God.

These truths are simple but also profound. For they are God's words of wisdom and not man's feeble philosophy. Paul wrote them to a group of struggling new Christians. These babes-in-the-faith had concerns about death, questions about the second coming of Christ. What happens to believers still living when Christ returns, and where are the beloved dead now? From these words of Paul consider the following truths.

THERE IS A BURDEN TO BEAR

The first is this: There really is a burden to bear. Many people ignore or deny death. As God's people in Christ, you ponder death as one embraced by the Savior. *(Name)* is no longer here among us. Such is your burden because her life has impacted your lives in important ways. Now you face life lacking the earthly fellowship of this great saint, whose presence was so welcome and whose zest for life was most contagious. Whenever I visited her recently, I always gained more than I could possibly give. That is a common observation among pastors.

Your loss has yielded many tears. This is not a weakness of faith, as some believe it to be. Stoicism is not a godly virtue. But your grief at this time takes on a different style than the grief of those who have no hope. St. Paul admonishes us,

44

"We do not want you to be uninformed, brothers, about those who are asleep, that you may not grieve as others do who have no hope" (1 Thess 4:13). Paul does not assert that grief is wrong, but rather admonishes us that grief without hope is not the way of God's people.

YOU AND YOUR SECOND FAMILY

There is a burden to bear. In Christian love within the family you freely give each other your strength. You bear your burdens as a family knit together by Christ. Together you converse, cry, remember, and laugh. You share experiences in your lives through which our departed sister offered love. But there is still more help available. By God's grace you also have a second family to which you may turn. It is the Church, the living Body of Christ. And it is no small blessing. *(Name)* loved the Church. She, too, was a member of Christ's body, and a member of great value at that. By her we have all been blessed.

"Bear one another's burdens, and so fulfill the law of Christ" (Gal 6:2). God's people do this as part of their Christian calling. During her life, *(name)* proved a ready ear to the discouraged, an open heart to the sad. After her example open now your arms and hearts to one another. You may never find all the right words. Nor do you need them. For your Christian love, caring, sharing, and burden-bearing will find many ways to express itself. Yes, at this time and on this occasion, there is a burden to bear, but we do not bear it alone.

THERE IS A HOPE TO SHARE

Now since we grieve not as others without hope, I offer this second profession of faith. While there is a burden to bear, there is a hope to share. That hope takes into account the future of our departed sister as well as the faith by which we, who remain on this earth a while longer, walk the pathway of this life. In the Bible the word *hope* is not defined as a wistful desire, as something that may or may not come to pass. Biblical hope is absolutely true. Thus this sure, certain hope has become for our dear sister *(name)* the reality of life forever in heaven. But it also addresses you and me with implications for our eternal future.

First, we know with assurance where *(name)* is spending eternity. She is in heaven's home! If this dear saint has left a will there can be nothing within it as precious as this legacy. Can there be a greater legacy than knowing she is cradled in Christ? Never! *(Name)* was a gracious person, an outstanding human being. But our assurance of her salvation is not based on her goodness. It is based on what God has done for her. *(Name)* believed she was a sinner who needed God's grace.

In word and deed she confessed that Jesus lived a holy life in her stead and died an innocent death on a cross she should have borne. She always had that vision of a Lord whose lavish love drove Him to endure the pain of a vile and lonely cross! She shared with me on several occasions that if she were the only person who needed saving, Christ would have done it just for her. Yet her faith also perceived that Jesus would never be caught dead in a grave! So, as the Bible affirms, she believed that because Christ rose again from the dead, she would be a shoo-in for resurrection as He so pledged her. And how did she get such a faith?

(Name) believed that the seed of salvation was first planted in the soil of her heart when God's Word and Spirit, in the water of Baptism, became God's claim on her soul. She was His property. As she faced her daily task of walking with God, His Word and Sacrament kept her firm in that resolve. It gave her a strength for life and a hope as she met death, so much so that you can now hope through your tears. For one so firmly entrenched in God's grace, there is no doubt that she is forever with the Lord, part of that great cloud of witnesses that cheers us on as we daily fight the good fight of faith.

As for You

(Name) is with the Lord. Are you? Are you walking as yet by faith with Him now as she led you to do? Are you resolved to remain clutched in the caring hands of the Good Shepherd? For if that is true, there will be a family reunion more glorious than any you could possibly experience here on earth. Jesus Christ will host that reunion. One of *(name's)* urgent desires is that we continue to admonish one another to hold fast your faith and crown. Remember Paul's reminder: "And so we will always be with the Lord" (1 Thess 4:17). That, in any event, has always been the final goal of your family.

There is a hope to share. *(Name)* is with Christ, and so shall we be someday. What a saga of salvation, which calls for your faithfulness as you finish out life. That, too, like sharing the burden of the hour, is a mutual task of God's people. The last sentence in Paul's words about death and resurrection says the following: "Therefore encourage one another with these words" (1 Thess 4:18). Such is our blessed task.

There Is a Lord to Care

This brings me to the final profession or divine truth I am privileged to proclaim. Throughout these ensuing days, weeks, and months of grief and sorrow, there will always be at your side a Lord to care. Such is His promise and nature. You will find Him, of course, in the words of Scripture you may have memorized. You will find Him in the Bible you read and the hymns you sing based on that

Bible. You will find Him feeding you His body and blood in the bread and wine of the blessed Sacrament, as life tends to absorb our strength of faith. Do not refuse or ignore the power that comes from God. It has a purpose especially now. Endurance!

So You Have the Power to Endure

Know that the Lord's care for you gives you power by God's grace to wait for that great reunion of the saints when Christ comes in glory. He promises, "Cast your burden on the LORD, and He will sustain you; He will never permit the righteous to be moved" (Ps 55:22). "I am coming soon. Hold fast what you have, so that no one may seize your crown" (Rev 3:11). There are so many other words of Scripture that also bear testimony to the love of God.

Given what God has told us, there is a burden to bear, a hope to share, and a Lord to care. Leave this place not having endured a tragedy, but celebrating a triumph only God could author. The hero is Jesus Christ. Trust in Him, grateful for this departed sister and all the blessed memories we keep and grateful for the living Lord who gave her to us as a precious gift. How safe she is in the arms of the Savior. How blest we are to grieve in holy style. May Jesus' peace, power, joy, and love be with you all—in your minds and in your hearts and in your understanding.

Rev. Brian R. Dill

Sermon for Paul, a Suicide

1 Peter 1:3

Some of us have worshiped in this five-walled building before, and some of us have never even seen the inside of this building. Perhaps some of us haven't worshiped God in a long, long time. But we are all here today, with all our varied backgrounds and different ages and perhaps diverse faiths, because we have been drawn by a common tragedy: the death of a young man who we felt had a long and happy and fulfilling life before him. We are all here because we have a single purpose. We want to share our comfort with the family struck by this tragedy. We want to remember this young man who touched our lives in different ways, whose death has touched us all the same—with shock and sadness.

In the name of the Christ, who lived and died for us and rose again, I greet all of you who are here today. I greet you as fellow pilgrims who are traveling through this life toward a life to come. I especially greet you members of the bereaved family, and I pray that you may receive a special measure of God's mercy and grace and peace in these days. I know that God will grant that, for His promises are sure. I join all of you in this hour of worship to seek words of comfort from our gracious God, and to remember with you a handsome and spirited young man—a son, a brother, a friend, a young man full of life and a zest for living. Who today will not remember tennis and golf and a Rolex watch and a hot Mustang? We are here to remember Paul, who was a gift from God to us for eighteen years.

When tragedy enters the life of a believer in Christ, the Christian turns immediately to God and His Word, for only in the eternal love of God can understanding and comfort and strength be found. We turn to God today because He loves us forever, and we know that He and He alone can provide the patience and the comfort and the strength we so desperately need.

If God had no message for us in such a time of disaster and grief—if He did not reach out, offering us love and hope—we would be tempted to turn against God and blame Him for the anguish that has come to us. I suppose when all of us heard the shocking news of Paul's death, we immediately asked the age-old question, "Why?" Why did God let this kind of thing happen? Why didn't He stop the process?

Such questions will never be answered fully this side of eternity, because we can never ever understand what goes on in a person's mind, especially in the extremity of death. In a time of perplexity such as this, it is good that we not become preoccupied with God's governance or the reasons behind what has happened. Nor should we—family member or college friend or fraternity brother—ever assume guilt that is not ours by thinking something we said or did might have made the difference, or that something we did not say or do would have changed the outcome. This kind of assumed guilt is not just; it is not fair to ourselves or to the memory of Paul.

Instead, we ought to concentrate on the fact that Paul was a gift from God for eighteen years. And those eighteen years of life far outweigh the event of this weekend. Let the fact that Paul was God's gift fill your hearts and your minds this day. As long as you live, be thankful to God for the eighteen years Paul walked with us.

You can bear the burden of this sorrow if you remember God's word to us today: "According to His great mercy, He has caused us to be born again to a living hope through the resurrection of Jesus Christ from the dead" (1 Pet 1:3). When Peter wrote these words, he likely was thinking of how his readers recently had been baptized. At this moment we think of the miraculous new birth in Holy Baptism that God gave to Paul.

Baptism says God has chosen us, and His door and His arms are open wide to us. He takes us—sinful people that we are—and draws us into the very life and death and resurrection of Jesus. All that Jesus did for us becomes ours in Baptism. He died in our place to pay the penalty for our sins. His death counts for us. Then He rose from the dead, and He shares with us His life with God that doesn't stop at the grave. The new birth in Baptism is birth to a life of hope, because it unites us with Jesus Christ, who rose from the dead. That's why Peter wrote, "He has caused us to be born again to a living hope." That hope transcends this earth and fills all eternity with glory. That hope of salvation belongs to all baptized believers. God's grace is powerful enough and quick enough to forgive each of us who trusts in Christ, regardless of our circumstances. If we didn't believe that, none of us could sleep at night.

Now hear this again: "Blessed be the God and Father of our Lord Jesus Christ!" These words are all the more remarkable because they were originally spoken not in days of sunshine, but in days when the persecuted Church faced darkness, suffering, and anguish. It is a miracle of faith when an afflicted person speaks such words during a time of trouble and uncertainty.

God helped those persecuted believers to praise Him. And He will help you say those words as you recall that God has touched you with the finger of His love through the life of Paul at least four major times: when God gave Paul life and he was born; when God brought Paul into the family of His Church by giving him the new birth of salvation and the forgiveness of sins in Holy Baptism; when God's Spirit led Paul to confess Christ publicly in his confirmation vows before this altar; and now, this past weekend, when God used that tragic event to bring you closer to each other and to Himself.

> Blessed be the God and Father of our Lord Jesus Christ! According to His great mercy, He has caused us to be born again to a living hope through the resurrection of Jesus Christ from the dead. (1 Pet 1:3)

God keep you strong in the faith and secure in the everlasting love of Christ.

Rev. John D. Fritz

Weddings

One Forever and for Good

Genesis 2:18–24; 1 Corinthians 12:31–13:8; John 15:12–17

Dear *(name)* and *(name)*,

There is an apocryphal story about Adam and Eve that relates to our first reading for today. According to the story, one day Adam worked into the early evening in the Garden of Eden, not realizing in that pleasant environment that the sun had begun to set and that he was late for dinner. Upon arriving home he encountered an irate wife standing in the doorway. Eve said to him accusingly, "Adam, where have you been? Have you been out with another woman?" Adam replied, "Don't be silly, Eve. I couldn't have been out with another woman. There is no other woman." Eve could not argue with her husband's logic but neither could she deny her feelings. So she waited until Adam fell asleep soundly that night and then she counted his ribs.

Of all the references to marriage in the Bible, the Genesis 2 creation account is one of my favorites. It reveals a God who is extremely sensitive to us humans and intimately involved with His creation. It portrays a God who not only gives us the world, the beasts of the field, the birds of the air, and the creatures in the water, but who gives us one another as well.

If you asked me to summarize in one word the purpose for which God gives a woman to a man and a man to a woman, the word I would choose is the word *love*. God gives people to people in order that they may love one another. There is another word that, for all practical purposes, means the same as love. That is the word *serve*. God gives people to people so that they may serve one another.

On a day such as today, I doubt that the word I chose to describe God's intention for you surprises you. Love is in the air in this building. The two of you look at each other lovingly. The music is lovely, the flowers are beautiful, your families are supportive, and your friends don't look bad either. The setting is almost idyllic, like being in the Garden of Eden. You are surrounded by signs and symbols and feelings of love. It is enough to make you think that loving each other for the rest of your lives will be as easy as falling off a slippery log.

The Scriptures, however, speak not of sentimental love or emotional love but of a love that is intentional and self-giving. In the Epistle, Paul admonished the Corinthians to practice self-sacrificing love. He wrote of a love that is patient and kind, not jealous or boastful, neither arrogant nor rude. "Love . . . does not insist on its own way; it is not irritable or resentful; it does not rejoice at wrongdoing, but rejoices with the truth" (1 Cor 13:5–6). Paul urges us to love one another with a strong love that "bears all things, believes all things, hopes all things, endures all things" (v. 7).

Similarly, the Gospel opens with the words of Jesus: "This is My commandment, that you love one another as I have loved you" (Jn 15:12). Christ's love was anything but sentimental. It was the love of tough decisions that drove Him to wrestle against satanic powers, which tempted Him to forego the cross and to serve Himself rather than die for your sins, for mine, and for the sins of the whole world. The Savior's love committed Him wholeheartedly to doing His Father's will, which included the cross. To love others as Christ has loved us, we must offer the most we have to give: our entire life.

(*Name*), I hope you know that (*Name*) is not going to be as easy to love every day of your marriage as she is today. One morning you are going to roll over in bed and remember the disagreement you had the day before. You will risk opening just one eye as you look at your wife lying next to you, and you will ask, "Lord, is this the woman You gave to me on the day of my marriage? Is this the woman with whom You want me to spend the rest of my life? Do I really have to love her just as Christ loved me and His entire Bride, the Church, and gave Himself up for her on the cross? Do I really have to sacrifice myself for her?" It is not going to be as easy to love her that morning as it is this afternoon.

(*Name*), your husband, too, is not going to be as easy to love every day of your marriage as he is today. One morning you are going to look beyond the lump in the bed that is your husband to the pile of crumpled laundry he has left lying on the floor instead of in the hamper, and you are going to say, "Lord, in all of Your mixing and matching of husbands and wives, are You certain this is not more of a mix than a match? Are You certain this is the man with whom You want me to spend the rest of my life? Do I really have to follow those words of Jesus, 'This is My commandment, that you love one another as I have loved you' (Jn 15:12)?"

Sooner or later you are going to hurt each other and disappoint each other. You will think the unkind thought and speak the hurting word. Then Satan will tempt you to turn away from each other and seek a seemingly easier solution than extending to each other the forgiveness you both need to make your relationship whole again.

Where can you find the strength you will need to resist Satan at such times? How will you be able to keep the vows you are making to each other today? How will you find the humility and grace to forgive and sacrifice over and over?

The answer to those questions lies in the words of Jesus immediately before the Gospel for today. Before giving His commandment that we should love one another, Jesus said, "I am the vine; you are the branches. Whoever abides in Me and I in him, he it is that bears much fruit, for apart from Me you can do nothing" (Jn 15:5). The ability to remain one with each other comes from remaining one with Jesus Christ. Your marriage makes you one flesh with each other; Jesus became flesh not only to dwell among us, but to give His flesh for our life and to live in us in such a fashion that we are never alone. As husband and wife, you are not in your marriage relationship alone. You are one not only with each other, but with your Savior, Jesus Christ.

When emotional love fails you and sentimental love is not enough to sustain you, then cling to your Baptism, through which you have put on the Lord Jesus Christ and have received the benefit of His life, death, and resurrection. Because of your Baptism, sin is not your master; Christ is. You can affirm in words and actions the love of Christ, which is the will of God for your life together as husband and wife.

When you are tempted to turn away from each other, recall what happens when you come to the Lord's Table to receive Christ's body and blood. Here the life of the Vine flows into us branches, so that He remains in us and we in Him. The body and blood of Jesus give you the forgiveness of your sins and the power to forgive each other just as God, for Christ's sake, forgives you.

As if this were not enough, I have more good news for you today. Paul's letter to the Ephesians tells us to be subject to one another out of reverence for Christ. After addressing himself to husbands and wives, telling them how each is to serve the other, he quoted those beautiful words from Genesis that we read at the beginning of this service: "Therefore a man shall leave his father and mother and hold fast to his wife, and the two shall become one flesh." Then Paul adds, "This mystery is profound, and I am saying that it refers to Christ and the church" (Eph 5:31–32). Your Baptism into Christ and your reception of His Supper unite you not only to Jesus Christ but also to the whole communion of saints. There is great power in the fact that you are not the only branches connected to the vine of Jesus Christ; there are many others connected to Him as well from whom you can draw strength and support.

One of the greatest mistakes most Americans make about marriage is considering it to be a private affair. I want you to know that what is taking place here today is not simply a matter between you two. Your marriage belongs first of all to God, who created you, redeemed you, and gave you to each other. It belongs to your parents, who have invested themselves in you and sustained you to this moment. It belongs to your friends, who honor you by their presence. It belongs to your congregation and to me. And I pledge to you, no matter where you are or where I am, if ever there is anything I can do to help your marriage, you can call upon me. I will be available to you and do all I can to help you keep the vows you make today.

If you live together in Christ's love and stay connected to Him, His promise to you is that your marriage will bear fruit. I am confident that the most important guest attending your wedding today—Jesus Christ—will remain a welcomed person in your marriage, and so your marriage will be a blessing to both of you, to the community in which you live, to the place where you work, to your congregation, and to our world. Together as you remain connected to Christ, you will not only be one forever, you will also be one for good. Amen.

Rev. George F. Lobien

Walking Side by Side

Genesis 2:18–24

A wedding is a time for family and friends to gather with a bridal couple to witness their marriage vows and to give them encouragement and support. However, we must never forget that it is a time of worship, a time to ask God's blessing on the couple He is joining together and to celebrate that God has promised to be a part of their life's journey. This worship service offers us the opportunity to give thanks to God for the gift He gives to us in marriage and provides a teaching opportunity for the pastor to speak of the values of marriage and the role that God plays in our relationships. The wedding service also provides the entrée to build bridges for reaching people who may not be inclined to frequent a house of worship under other circumstances. While the text and the occasion may not provide the context for a full Law/Gospel message, we do have the opportunity to plant seeds by speaking of the love of Jesus, His gift of forgiveness, and His desire to be part of our lives on a daily basis.

There were no words, at least no words that I could hear. But the way they looked at each other and the way they held each other's hand told a story of their life together. They moved slowly, but with grace and dignity as they strolled through the courtyard at the mall. They appeared to be well into their 80s. What I noticed was not so much their age as their obvious concern for each other. Occasionally, as they looked in the shop windows, she would glance at him with a twinkle in her eye as if to say, "You're my man and I love you." He in turn would smile a well-practiced smile and with only a look reply, "I know, and I love you too." They were obvious partners, friends, and lovers. Each had something to offer to the relationship as they walked side by side through the courtyard of a busy mall, and side by side along a lifetime journey of love.

As they walked, they told a story for anyone who would simply take the time to watch. It was a story without words. If words were necessary, the words could doubtless fill many chapters. These chapters would recall times of challenge and joy, struggle and success. The story began some sixty years ago in North Dakota the summer he worked for her father on the family farm. We can only imagine what details their story might have included. First, perhaps, their eyes met. Later, it might have been, they mustered the courage actually to talk to each other. Well, she did more talking than he. Soon they would be side by side at every church social and every county fair. They married not quite two years later, the July after she finished high school.

Their early years together were not easy, but neither seemed to mind. Times were tough in rural America in those days, and they had to struggle just to keep food on the table. But they succeeded by working together, side by side. Soon they were presented with another challenge, the challenge of moving from being a couple to being a family. As the first of their children began to arrive, they sometimes had to sacrifice what they wanted so that their young children could have new shoes or a warm coat during those cold and windy North Dakota winters. However, what this family lacked materially they made up for in warmth, humor, and tenderness.

It was about this time that they decided to move west. Perhaps their children were reaching school age. Now, their evenings were filled with church and school events and with helping the young ones with homework. The years continued, and they finished the elementary school portion of their family history and entered the adolescent chapter. This was the most challenging period of their life together. Their parenting skills were tested virtually every day.

But before long it was time for graduation, marriage, and new directions for their children, who were now young adults. In this chapter, the couple launched their children into journeys of their own as they established their own families. For our couple it was a time of writing a new chapter for themselves too. It was a time of reconnecting, but in a new way. Now they had time once again to center their lives on each other. It was a time of making readjustments, renewing old interests, and reprioritizing their time. To them it may have seemed like just yesterday that they were changing diapers and getting kids ready for school. Now they were thinking about such things as vacations, travel, and where they might like to retire.

The couple I saw in the mall had a story. They could tell us much about what it means to be married—to be partners who walk side by side, making the journey of love. This is the kind of partnership God intended for us in marriage. But marriage is not only our story; it is God's story too. Marriage is about God's gifts of life and love, God's blessings of companionship and forgiveness. The marriage of two people is a story with many pages filled with dreams and disappointments, tangles and triumphs. Marriage as God intended it is not a onetime event or a onetime commitment. It is instead a series of commitments. It is adjusting and readjusting, tuning and fine-tuning a partnership. It is walking side by side. This was God's plan from the very beginning, as the first steps were taken in the first marriage.

Genesis 2 tells the story of another couple—the first couple to begin the journey of marriage. This time we know their names—they were called Adam and Eve. They, too, were partners. God said, "It is not good that the man should be alone; I will make him a helper fit for him" (Gen 2:18). The word used for "helper" does not mean an assistant or someone who is subordinate or dependent. This helper is a gift from God—a helper who is an equal, a partner, a companion, a trusted friend who brings mutual support. There was no other created being that could be all of this for Adam, so God made one who was suitable. To make sure that this helper was exactly right, God took a rib from man and used this as the material to create woman. Rabbis of long ago said that woman was not taken from man's head to be lord over him, nor from his feet to be walked on, but from his side to walk next to him. Adam and Eve were created to walk side by side.

In marriage "a man shall leave his father and his mother and hold fast to his wife, and they shall become one flesh" (Gen 2:24). In this relationship two become one—but not in the sense of losing themselves or giving up their individuality. The elderly couple I saw in the mall that day was united. They worked and functioned as a unit. They were obviously a team. But they were also very much individuals. Each had something to contribute as they walked side by side, supporting each other throughout their journey, year after year, chapter after chapter.

This couple had a story to tell as they slowly but gracefully strolled through the courtyard of a busy mall. They were God's gift to each other. And you, too, as you stand before the altar of God today, are a gift to each other. You, too, will write many chapters as you walk side by side. No chapter will be exactly the same. In your story there will be movement and growth. There will be surprises. There will be adjustments and readjustments. You may just have come to understand what it means to be a couple when you need to learn to be parents. You may gain skills in parenting young children and then need to adjust to being parents of school-age children. And the plot continues. You see, the story that you have written to this point in your acquaintance—a story of love and commitment—is one that you will continue to write. You will add new dimensions. There will be new developments. There will be movement, changes, and challenges as you walk together side by side.

Today you are beginning your journey. It won't always be easy (just ask any older couple at the mall). There may be times when you let each other down. There may be days when you become angry and say things you wish you had never said. There may be times on the road when you are not a good traveling companion. But be assured that you will never be alone on the road. God, who brought you together, will always be walking with you. Remember, this is His story too.

His story begins with Adam and Eve, created in His image but soon overcome by the harsh reality of sin and death. Yes, God spoke words of life, but His people chose ruin, separation from all that is good and holy and perfect. Yet God did not end the story there. He spoke His word of promise once more, the promise of a Savior, the promise of redemption from eternal ruin.

"When the fullness of time had come," writes St. Paul, "God sent forth His Son, born of woman, born under the law, to redeem those who were under the law, so that we might receive adoption as sons" (Gal 4:4–5). Jesus is the fulfillment of God's promise, God's story. In His death and resurrection for our salvation, He brings to a glorious climax the story of God's love and mercy. The Lord Jesus shows us His Father's heart, a heart filled with tender forgiveness. He gives His life that we might live as God's chosen people, God's dearly loved children. It is the story I love to tell, the story we love to hear. It is your story today, as you begin your life together in His name.

Perhaps one day, many years from now, after many chapters of your life have been written, you may be walking along in a mall and someone will look at you and see a story, a story without words, a story of love and forgiveness. They will see a couple walking side by side through all the troubles of life. They will see in you a Savior who has guided you every step of the journey and who promises heaven at the end of your days. It's your storybook, but it's really His story. May God bless you richly as you trust in Jesus and walk with Him in your marriage.

Rev. Philip E. Streufert

Three Commitments in Marriage

Genesis 2:21–24

Do any of the words in the text bother you? Let me explain a few of them. *Man* in the text is not male. It is *adam*, which means "from the dust." In Gen 5:2 it says, "Male and female He created them, and He blessed them and named them Man." It is also not a "rib." The word in Hebrew is a word for "section," or "part."

The picture is that God took the first human and divided it into two. So God made two different persons, "male" and "female," "ish" and "ishshah." Then the Hebrew text has Adam look at Eve and say, "Wow! This is all right! This is bone of my bones and flesh of my flesh! I can live with this!" (paraphrase).

Then the text reunites what God just divided. The two once again become "one flesh" in their marriage. The word "unite" literally means to "cleave" or "adhere." The two become one, dedicated and committed to a common life.

That's what marriage is. It is loyalty. I personally don't like to talk about love. It is such a frothy, misused word. We love everything from pizza to football to a spouse. I think a clearer word to use in marriage is loyalty, adhering and cleaving to each other as "bone of my bones and flesh of my flesh" (v. 23).

Loyalty to the Oneness

I'd like to talk about marriage in three sentence pairs—words I'd like you to say to each other this day. The first is, "*(Name)*, I need you." The reply is, "*(Name)*, I'll be there." That's loyalty. It's not promising to be perfect. Each of you has failings and weaknesses. If you haven't revealed them yet, you soon will. As I told you in marriage preparation, marriage will bring out the best in you and it will bring out the worst in you. You know you need each other. You promise to be there.

That's the way God commits Himself to us. He did it in your Baptism. He said, "I will be your God. You will be My child. Whatever happens I will never leave you or forsake you. Although you are faithless, I will not be faithless because I cannot deny Myself." You can live in that unfailing promise of God. You can draw on that strength and be that strength for each other.

Respect to the Individual

The second sentence pair is "*(Name)*, I am different." And the reply is: "*(Name)*, I like you." You become one, but you are different. We discussed this also in our marriage preparation. Women and men are different. Our needs and ways and thinking are different.

When you light the marriage candle in just a few minutes, you will leave the two individual candles lit. While you become one in marriage, you are still two individuals, two different people. You commit yourselves to help the other blossom and grow. You tell each other: "I want you to be all that you can be."

You love and respect each other in your differences. You enjoy your differences and revel in the mystery of a new creation under God. You say today and in all the days to come: "Wow! This is good. I'm going to enjoy this."

That is the way God created you. He has a vision for your life in His service both as individuals and as a couple. You will fail in that vision time and again. Yet your God never gives up on you. He will always be there to piece you back together both as individual persons and as a couple.

God likes what He made. He says "Wow! I like you and all you can be. You are special and wonderful in My eyes." He rejoices that you can discover that boundless beauty He has hidden in each of you.

Forgiveness and Trust from God

The third sentence pair: "*(Name)*, I'm sorry" and "*(Name)*, I'll forgive." Forgiveness is the glue that keeps a marriage together. You trust the relationship enough to show your vulnerability. You trust your partner's love enough to ask their forgiveness.

That's how we are with God. We trust His love. We know that "while we were still sinners, Christ died for us" (Rom 5:8). We recognize our faults and failings and are bold to confess them. We know He will forgive and help. The price for our sins has been paid. We can walk in newness of life. Our God is always ready to give us a new start when we repent. We let that love of God fill our hearts to overflowing. We revel in it together and share it with each other. Marriage is the ongoing celebration of forgiveness.

These are the sentence pairs for this day:

"I need you." "I'll be there."
"I'm different." "I like you."
"I'm sorry." "I forgive you."

And they lived happily ever after.

Rev. Herbert E. Hoefer

Marriage: God's Picture of Himself for Us

Matthew 19:4–8

Today, probably at this very moment, all over the world marriages are beginning. In gatherings much like this one, men and women are standing side by side, surrounded by family and friends who are there to witness what is, by any measure, an important event in the lives of those about to enter the holy estate of marriage. Why is this such a universal occurrence? For as long as humankind has inhabited this planet, marriage has been a part of the picture. And now, you are here before the altar of God's church and before His people to say your solemn vows of holy marriage.

Today you are stepping into a continuum of history dating back to the very beginning of human history.

Marriage is the first human relationship ever established. God established it because He knew it was not good for people to be alone. In a very real sense our heavenly Father has "custom-designed" woman for man and man for woman. Therefore, marriage between a man and a woman is a wonderful creation of God.

MARRIAGE IS THE EXPRESSION OF GOD'S WILL

In God's great wisdom He has divinely designed husband and wife to be the very expression of His will. We are divinely designed to be a perfect "fit" for one another. We are designed to fit each other emotionally, physically, spiritually, and intellectually. When you join together in marriage this day you will become more as one.

Marriage, therefore, is an age-old and sacred practice. Despite all the voices in our world that denigrate marriage, it is right that you are here! Despite the curses our society chooses when it opts for easy divorce and a distorted picture of marriage that represents it to be less than what God designed it to be, what you are about to do is absolutely ordained by God! You already know that, don't you? That is why you have chosen to be here before the altar of God.

The union you are about to enter is a sacred mystery. The language of Jesus in this text is puzzling from a human perspective. How can two become one? God is describing a totally new way of relating as human beings. He is not describing two independent people who have merely chosen to live together, but rather the creation of an entirely new entity, comprised of two people, who are taking sacred vows to live as a new kind of sacred unit. You are becoming a "we," and not just a pair of "I's."

In a very real way, God has created a human relationship that gives us a picture of Himself. There is the sacred mystery of the Holy Trinity. Three persons—Father, Son, and Holy Spirit—yet one God. Then consider the mystery of Jesus Christ Himself. In Christ there are two natures—divine and human—but one person. And now in marriage, two people become one flesh.

In the holiness of marriage we can begin, then, to comprehend the graciousness of God Himself. Here is a view of God personified. Christ was willing to give up the glory of God to become a man. He was willing to become the servant of another because of our desperate need for a restored relationship with Him, a relationship that had been broken by humanity's sinful rebellion. Christ was willing to sacrifice His life for the sake of His beloved people.

Marriage, too, is a place of considering the other person's needs ahead of your own, a place of mutual servanthood for the sake of another, a place of personal sacrifice for the love of another. The more you look at the love of Christ for us, the more you will understand your own marriage and how marriage works. If you wish to learn how to love one another as husband and wife in such a way that the quality of your love continues to grow with the passage of time, then you must learn more about the love of God in Christ Jesus. God is love, and He will teach you what love truly is.

As you begin this mysterious and sacred journey today, remember that it is God, the Creator of this holy and blessed institution of marriage, who stands ready to show you how to live confidently in His love and His forgiveness together for as long as you live on this earth.

This is a time blessed by God and established in His name. Find your mutual joy in the journey with Him.

Rev. Richard A. Bolland

A Love Song of Praise

Romans 15:5–7

We are grateful for the beautiful music and musicians here today. A wedding without music would be a dull and lifeless event and I am sure your new home will be filled with tunes. The biblical text you have chosen is appropriate: "Together you may with one voice glorify the God and Father of our Lord Jesus Christ" (Rom 15:6). We gather to pray that your marriage will be a love song of praise to God.

That was God's idea in the very beginning. Genesis tells about it. At the end of each day of God's creative work, He took a look at His handiwork and said, "It is good; it is good" (see Genesis 1). Until the sixth day, when God stood back, took a look at His creation, and said, "It is not good that the man should be alone" (Gen 2:18).

Something more was needed. Adam was like a perfect melody line. It sounds good, but more is needed. So God went back to work. He took a rib of Adam and from it made another person who was the same, but different. She was a new creation in the same key, but a different melody. When God brought the two of them together they made an intriguing counterpoint and beautiful harmony. And the three of them together—God, man, woman—were a veritable symphony. God said this is good: "A man shall leave his father and his mother and hold fast to his wife, and they shall become one flesh" (Gen 2:24).

Sin Spoils the Harmony

Sadly, Adam and Eve took their eyes off the conductor and decided to go their own way. The harmony was disrupted. As they drifted away from God, they drifted away from one another. We still see the results today, especially in family life, where spouse battles spouse, siblings fight, and children engage in power struggles with their parents. Now it's not the harmony that matters, but the self.

In the hardware store last Saturday, I witnessed two incidents that illustrate this disharmony. First, in the aisle, I heard a man and son loudly putting down the wife and mother because she didn't understand something about construction. Then at the checkout counter, I heard a woman loudly putting down her husband because he didn't use the 10-percent-off coupon, and she had to come back to get her $2 discount. I asked myself, Why? Why would that father and son speak so condescendingly to someone they presumably love? Why would a wife belittle her husband?

Sin ruins God's perfect harmony in marriage. Each person cares about himself or herself; each wants to dominate; each is concerned about his or her perspective; neither cares about the marriage. Each seeks to sing a solo, and the harmony is lost.

CHRIST RESTORES THE HARMONY

But God's love is such that it could not let discord prevail. He would do whatever necessary to put things back together, to overcome disharmony, even to the point of sacrificing His Son. Jesus says, "Abide in Me and bear much fruit." He puts us back in touch with God and leads us to change. When we trust in Christ, God looks on us through a cross-shaped window. Our sins are forgiven because they were paid for by Jesus' death on the cross. God looks at us and says, "It is good."

A husband at peace with God takes the focus off himself to build up his wife. Likewise, a woman at peace with God is at peace with herself and her marriage. Both of them can focus on their Christ-bound relationship. Each can say: God will take care of me; therefore, I can attend to the harmony. When they become discouraged, the assurance of God's presence and help gives them confidence to begin again. When sin disrupts their life together, forgiveness renews it. In Christ they have the power to say, "I'm sorry." And in Christ they have the power to say, "I forgive." With His forgiveness, Christ helps the music return.

On behalf of those gathered, we are here today to be your backup group. We want to support your marriage song with prayers and blessings and words of encouragement.

As Paul prayed for the Church in Rome, so first we pray for the Spirit to give you patience and perseverance in your home. The music doesn't happen overnight. You must become accustomed to many things. Luther once said that after being married for some time he was still surprised to wake up and find pigtails on the pillow next to his. There are many surprises coming—not all of them so delightful. But you can adjust with patience and perseverance from the Spirit. When the music is good, when it seems most effortless, you know that a lot of effort has gone into practice.

Second, we pray with Paul that the God of encouragement would send you His Spirit to minister to one another. Jesus promises: "Where two or three are gathered in My name, there am I among them" (Mt 18:20). You two are the Church in your home. Speak God's promises to one another. Tell each other of His goodness and greatness. Pray for one another. Lead one another to the Table, where He refreshes His people with holy food.

Finally, let Christ sing the lead. Follow Him in His song of love. Let your marriage be a ministry to others. As you are caught up in His mission together, you will be drawn closer to one another. And in this world, which is often filled with harsh discord, your marriage will echo the beautiful melody of God's love, a love song of praise.

Rev. Thomas M. Fields

Remember and Forget

1 Corinthians 13

(Names of couple), what a memorable day! A day long awaited. A day that took great planning and preparation. During this process, you both made an invitation list. A list of names—family members and friends—you wanted to attend this wedding to witness your vows to each other. You both wanted certain people here today. And you invited God to witness and bless this day. I commend you for inviting the right guest. You didn't keep your Savior off the list.

Before we continue, turn and face each other. Hold each other's hands and affirm your pledge of love in these words. Repeat after me. "I bind myself . . . to thee for life. . . . Having chosen as I pleased, . . . I will spend . . . the rest of my life . . . trying to please . . . the one I have chosen" (source unknown).

Turn toward me. *(Names of couple)*, you have chosen as you pleased. You chose to date. You chose to become engaged. And now, on this day, you have chosen to marry. On this day you stand before your Savior, your family, and your friends to affirm this vow: "I will try to please the one I have chosen."

I want to talk to you briefly about a successful marriage, a marriage that is God-pleasing, a marriage based on two things—remembering and forgetting.

REMEMBER

First, a successful marriage is based on remembering. *(Groom's name)*, as one man to another, there is one date you must remember every year without fail and that is *(today's date)*. All kinds of things will help both of you remember this date—video, pictures, wedding album, the ring on your finger.

Why is it so important to remember this date? Because it is the day you stood before your God, your Creator, your Redeemer, your Sanctifier, and pledged your love and faithfulness. It is the day you publicly affirmed, "I have chosen *(couple's names)* to be my lifelong companion." This date you invited God to witness your commitment to each other and to take an active part in your marriage. A successful marriage is based on remembering.

But on this day, God would also have you begin to forget. The Scripture you chose for this day is 1 Corinthians 13. A portion of that chapter on Christian love reads, "Love is patient and kind; love does not envy or boast; it is not arrogant or rude. It does not insist on its own way; it is not irritable or resentful; it does not rejoice at wrongdoing, but rejoices with the truth. Love bears all things, believes all things, hopes all things, endures all things" (1 Cor 13:4–7).

Be Forgetful!

This portion of Scripture has some wonderful things to say about a successful marriage. I want to focus on the phrase "Love . . . keeps no record of wrongs" (v. 5 NIV). Love is not only about remembering but also about forgetting—especially forgiving.

Your marriage may be made in heaven, but it will be lived on earth. Because we are sinful people by nature, there is one thing we do really well—sin. And the reality is that we hurt those we love most. There will be times when you will be hurt by the other's actions. That hurt will tempt you to forget your wedding vows and remember the pain.

There is one individual who does not want your marriage to succeed—the devil. He is the enemy of every family, and he will try to destroy your marriage. How? By causing you to forget what you are supposed to remember, and causing you to remember what you are supposed to forgive and forget. How can you have a successful marriage? By centering your relationship in Jesus Christ. The apostle Paul writes, "In [Christ] all things hold together" (Col 1:17).

Your Relationship with Jesus

Your Savior has a relationship with each of you. His relationship is based on two things—remembering and forgetting. He remembers your needs, your concerns, your dreams. He hears your prayers. He promises He will never leave you. He remembers. But He also forgets. He forgives and forgets your sin. He died for you on the cross and by that act declares that He keeps no record of your sins. When it comes to our sins, God has divine amnesia. Your Savior says today, "*(Names of couple)*, because I have kept no record of your wrongs, you also should keep no record of wrongs with one another."

It has been said, "The key to a successful marriage is to keep your eyes wide open before marriage and half closed after." During your life together, may your eyes be wide open and focused on the cross of Jesus Christ and closed to each other's sins. Do these two things in your marriage—remember this day and your commitment; forget each other's faults and failures, for love keeps no record of wrongs. May God bless you with His love and forever dwell in your home.

Rev. Paul W. Arndt

Love Never Fails

1 Corinthians 13:7–8a

My first church was located deep in the wetlands of southern Louisiana. Because I was a lonely bachelor, I quickly struck up a friendship with an elderly Cajun neighbor by the name of René Gravois.

René had grown up in deep poverty, but ambition had motivated him to become first the manager and then the owner of a sugar plantation. When I first met René, I thought he was either a bachelor or widower, since he was living alone.

But René was married. His wife was living in a nursing home. René met and fell in love with Suzette when he was but a hired hand on a plantation. She became his wife. And not only was she a hardworking partner, but she was also a Christian. She related the Good News of Jesus Christ to René. Through Suzette, René came to know Jesus Christ, our Lord and the world's only Savior.

Then one day Suzette told her husband, René, that she was going to have their baby. The two of them looked forward to the birth of what they both hoped would be the first of many children. Finally, the day arrived and Suzette gave birth to a healthy girl. But René's celebration was cut short when just a few days later Suzette suffered a massive emotional breakdown.

As days and weeks went by, René refused to leave his wife's side. He would read to her from their French Bible, pray for her, and encourage her. But she showed no signs of improvement. Finally, after months of silence, Suzette once again began to speak. But instead of speaking the sweet, tender words that René loved to hear from her, she hurled horrible threats and accusations at him, which cut his heart and wounded his soul.

Because of Suzette's violent nature, René had to place her in a nursing home. But every day he visited her. He would bring her the day lilies that grow so beautifully in southern Louisiana. He would tell her of their little girl. He would comb her hair, bathe her, wash her clothes, and tell her how much he looked forward to having her back as his loving wife and the mother of his child.

But weeks went by and no improvement came. René learned how to prepare the baby's food, bathe the baby, and be both mom and dad to the baby. As months went by, he learned how to press the little girl's dresses, comb her hair, and be both mom and dad to a little girl. As years went by, René taught their young lady how to dance and drive a car, and he learned how to be both mom and dad to a young woman.

From the beginning, René's family had urged him to forget Suzette, find a new wife, and marry again so his daughter could have a mother. And who would blame him for doing so? But René refused because, you see, he had a love for Suzette that "bears all things, believes all things, hopes all things, endures all things" (v. 7). And René would be the first to say that his enduring love came from the Christ he first learned about from Suzette.

Our culture, and our fallen human nature, do not have that kind of love. That kind of love can only come from outside ourselves—from above. Our human nature is sinful and selfish. Our society is corrupted with self-centeredness. People tell us that we shouldn't have to give of ourselves, only take. And so, when your husband lets you down, leave him. When your wife disappoints you, forget her.

But Jesus has a love for us that bears the insults of our rejection of Him, bears the injuries of our daily disobedience, and bears the disappointments of our habitual sins against Him. Jesus loves us with a love that doesn't take away but keeps on giving. He died in our place. He rose again. He gives us the forgiveness of our sins. He gives us peace with God; on the cross He was rejected by the Father in order to reconcile us to God permanently. He gives us eternal hope because He died for us and rose again on Easter morning.

The word in v. 7 (*stego*) that is translated "bears" originally meant in classical Greek "to cover over with a roof (*stege*) in order to shelter, keep dry, protect." A translation that makes use of that original image could be, "Love is like a roof with no leaks." It stands over you, protecting you from the elements, deflecting the rain, holding up under the weight of the snow. The love that Jesus has shown the whole world by His death and resurrection now reaches out to you. In your Baptism into Christ, in His Word, and in His Supper, His love encompasses you, covering and protecting you. And it is a love that stands firm over you, no matter what storms, hurricanes, tornados, or blizzards may strike. Through René, Jesus' love continues to cover and protect Suzette. May Jesus' love do the same through each of you.

Next, Paul says that love "believes all things, hopes all things." The word *pisteuo*, translated "believes," is the common New Testament word used for believing in Christ. He's talking about faith. Christian faith takes God at His Word—and His Word is Christ. René told me that when Suzette and he were trying to buy the plantation in the midst of the Great Depression, he would worry about how they were going to pay the bills. Suzette would then remind him of God's promise in Rom 8:28: "We know that for those who love God all things work together for good, for those who are called according to His purpose." God did see them through to own that plantation.

René never left Suzette, he said, because deep down he knew God would somehow—at some time—turn that horrible situation around. If Suzette were not restored in this life, certainly she would be in the life to come, and that is not too long to wait. Love believes that. It trusts and hopes for the best, knowing that things will get better, much better—if not on this earth, then certainly in heaven. Love knows that the troubles we may have to put up with in this world are brief in comparison to eternity.

That was the attitude of Jesus. He suffered many things during His earthly life. He endured the cross, believing and trusting the Father, even when He was forsaken. He knew that by carrying out the Father's plan of salvation He would redeem the entire human race. He was confident that the Father's love, at work in Him, would conquer all—even death, hell, and the devil. God's love in Christ has provided a blissful eternity, free of all the problems, big and small, that plague us in this life. Love believes that. And love is content to wait patiently until God fulfills all His promises. Let Jesus' love for you move you always to believe and trust like that.

Paul goes on to say that love "endures all things." Love goes through all things, not with whiny self-pity, but with a spirit of strength to conquer any problem. Again, that's the way Jesus lived. Heb 12:2 says, "For the joy that was set before Him [Jesus] endured the cross." Jesus went to the cross because He knew it was the only way to procure our salvation, and the fulfillment of His mission was the way to eternal joy. His joy was in bringing us joy. May each of you always find your greatest joy in bringing joy to the other.

In your married life there are going to be challenges, problems. There are going to be demanding times: friction when you are together, stress when you are apart. But you can endure it. Remember, Jesus promises you that from this day forward you will spend eternity together with Him. Maybe there will be some tight financial times ahead when the best that you can do for supper is boil up a delicious pot of Ramen noodles. But that's okay. Remember that Jesus promises to give you a banquet in heaven that will far surpass any banquet connected with this wedding. His promises will give you a love strong enough to endure all your problems.

Paul concludes by saying, "Love never ends" (v. 8a). Love makes it to the end. If I told you no more about René and Suzette, I'm sure that you'd leave here a little depressed about this story. For fifty years a man bore all things, believed all things, hoped for all things, and endured all things without any results. But something did happen in the end.

About a year before Suzette died, she began to change. She would smile when René came into the room. She would reach out to him. She began to speak those sweet words from long ago. Slowly, René got Suzette back. She came home. She got to see her granddaughter married. And shortly before Suzette died, René and Suzette got to go on the honeymoon they couldn't afford fifty years before.

None of those things would have happened if it were not for the fact that René had Christ's love for Suzette—love that "bears all things, believes all things, hopes all things, endures all things." Can you imagine how wonderful your life together will be with that kind of love? Jesus gives you a final promise: His love for you will never fail. In Him, your love for each other will never fail.

Rev. Daniel J. Decker

71

The Vocation of Marriage

Ephesians 4:1–3

So, are you ready for your new job, that is, your vocation as wife and husband? Today you are here because you have been invited by almighty God to begin this new vocation. The vocation of marriage is as demanding as it is exhilarating. The text provides the means for instructing you how to walk worthy of this precious invitation to be joined together as husband and wife.

WALK IN LOWLINESS

All of this is new for both of you and is unlike any other vocation you have ever had. It is a new walking because your relationship is new. The vows you make to each other this day establish a deep and abiding relationship between two persons that is unparalleled by anything else. To be sure, marriage will not change the uniqueness each of you brings into this relationship. God made each of you in a wonderfully special way. Each of you will put into this walk something of your-selves.

However, there are some attributes both of you should have. First, walk with lowliness. That does not mean to walk with your head down in a sad or self-pity-ing mode. Nor does it mean for one or the other of you to walk three steps behind the other. Rather, this refers to a style of interaction with each other. That you are now holding hands is good, and it is a good way to walk. To be soft or gentle with one another goes a long way in forming the bond of peace that God desires for your marriage. Softness does not imply being a Mr. or Mrs. Milquetoast. Neither one of you has to say "Yes, dear" to everything! But you may very well be gentle in how you say no. The tone of voice can often be more important than the actual words. As you walk and talk, may your words include words of faith, the faith you share in Jesus Christ. Walking in His ways does mean walking softly and with gen-tleness.

WALK WITH PATIENCE

Our text also talks of walking with patience. I like the word that the King James Version uses, namely, *long-suffering*. What on earth does it mean to be long-suf-fering in marriage? Does this mean "putting up with" the idiosyncrasies or even those irritating habits that the other person has? Not necessarily. But it does mean taking time to hear the whole story, getting all the facts before you respond.

(*Name*), that means you must wait until the sentence ends. When (*Name*) starts with, "Will you take . . ." don't automatically reach for the garbage. Maybe she'll want you to take her to the Rams game!

Patience means just that. In the midst of conflict, for example, choose your words carefully, always seeking reconciliation in the name of Jesus.

WALK WITH FORBEARANCE

Our text also exhorts you to bear with one another in love. Practice self-control. In order to create "unity of the Spirit" (v. 3), it is important to show restraint in your vocation of marriage. Rather than looking for your own way and having just your own plans, consider the other person. Make plans together. Requiring everything to be done to your satisfaction will surely bring problems in your marriage.

UNITY OF THE SPIRIT THROUGH THE BOND OF PEACE

These, then, are some of the ways to walk in this new vocation, this job, of marriage. It is just as important to consider the goal of your marriage. The text says to be "eager to maintain the unity of the Spirit in the bond of peace" (v. 3). In a very real sense, among your greatest tasks in marriage is to become what, by God's grace, you already are, namely, one in Christ. Is this unity for the two of you? Well, yes, to a degree. But even more so, it's the unity of you three! You two, with God in the midst of everything.

The walk on which you are embarking must always include the Lord Jesus. Because He died and rose again, you have forgiveness of sin. That profound truth gives people freedom to be in relationship with each other. When you find that you have not followed the guidelines of the first part of our text, you can trust in the forgiveness of God to bring you back on track. He walks with the two of you and has you in His loving care.

You can walk worthy of the vocation to which you have been called by the grace of God through the power of the Holy Spirit. It is good that you walk hand in hand; may your hands include the hand of God. He will give you strength, patience, love, and gentleness for living this vocation of marriage. Today and always we pray for His grace and guidance in your walk together.

Rev. Darryl A. Anderson

The Marks of Your Marriage: Wedding Sermon for a Widow and Widower

Ephesians 5:20

(*Name*) and (*Name*), friends and members of your family have gathered here this evening with you to express heartiest congratulations and God's richest blessings as you are joined together in holy marriage. It is fitting that you would select a portion from God's Holy Word to be shared at this, your wedding service, a special word that would hold before you the marks of your marriage. The apostle Paul by inspiration of the Holy Spirit writes, "Giving thanks always and for everything to God the Father in the name of our Lord Jesus Christ" (Eph 5:20).

HEARTS OF GRATITUDE TO GOD

What are the marks of your marriage? Your marriage is comprised of two thankful hearts. Both of you have expressed your gratitude to God in how the Lord has richly provided for you in the past. Both of you have experienced the sharp pain of grief and the loss of a loved one dear to you in death. The Lord had blessed you both in your previous marriages. You have witnessed how the Lord guides you through the trauma of grief.

Perhaps you may have questioned the apostle Paul's inspired advice to be always giving thanks for everything. But the experiences that the two of you individually have encountered have provided the settings for blessing you with growth in your relationship with your Savior, Jesus.

You have allowed yourselves to admit there is a hole of emptiness in your hearts. You have allowed each other to speak about that departed loved one. You have allowed yourselves to remind each other of God's love and care that He had provided for you in the past. You have allowed yourselves to remind each other that God's love and care do not stop but continue even now and throughout your lives. You are permeated by God's grace with thankful hearts.

There will be those times when we wonder about the "always" and the "everything." It is in those times of uncertainty, of doubt, of troubles and tempting despair that this word from the Lord's inspired writer brings to our minds the axiom that a thankful heart does not originate with itself. A thankful heart does

74

not even generate gratitude because we are commanded to be thankful. A thankful heart is a response to God's gracious working in our lives through our Lord Jesus Christ.

THRIVING ON THE PRESENCE OF JESUS CHRIST

That's why the marks of your marriage include thriving upon the presence of the Lord Jesus Christ. He serves as a witness to the vows that you will express to each other. As a witness He serves as a valuable help in enabling you to grow in your marriage relationship with each other.

Think of a triangle with Jesus as the top angle and husband and wife as the two bottom angles. As a husband and wife, you will grow closer in your relationship with each other by, first of all, being drawn into a close relationship with your Lord and Savior, Jesus Christ.

Jesus is present with His grace where He promises to be present, that is, in His Word and Sacrament. As your two families rejoice with you being joined together in marriage, so also does your Savior rejoice as He comes to be with you regularly through His Word and Sacrament. In that way, Jesus is present with you to feed you with His love that you may share His love with each other—the kind of love that expresses and lives God's forgiveness for your loved one.

Sin and selfishness do not vamoose when two become one in marriage, no matter what the age. When sin and selfishness continue to rear their ugly heads, the thankfulness in our hearts is found lacking. But when you as husband and wife together stand at the foot of the cross and are drawn to remember that Jesus died on the cross for your sins and rose from the dead to give you life in His name, then hearts are filled to the brim with thankfulness.

YOU ARE GOD'S GIFTS TO EACH OTHER

Thriving upon the presence of the Lord Jesus in your marriage means that you are God's gifts to each other. The Lord enables you to serve Him by serving each other in your sharing and in your enabling each other to grow. You help each other keep the eyes of faith on the Savior. You help each other with your compassion and care for each other. You help each other with the encouragement that God will never leave nor forsake His children. You remind each other that the Lord Jesus by His death and resurrection has primed your spiritual pump so that your lives together are responding with volumes of praise in thankful hearts thriving upon the presence of the Lord Jesus Christ.

(Name) and (Name), God's richest blessings to you as you begin your new life together in His name with His presence.

Rev. Kenneth J. Gerike

A Homily
for Jennifer and Scott

Ephesians 5:21

Whenever Christian people do something Christian, they are doing and telling the truth. Contrary to everything and everybody else around, they are, in truth, celebrating the fact that they are Christian and that being so makes a difference. Being a Christian makes a difference not only in the life to come but also in this life, in this world—today, as well as in all the tomorrows. So, as Christians, today you are doing and telling the truth before this altar and before all these people—and, above all, before God.

What you two are saying and doing is demonstrating to all of us that you know we are sinful human beings who are redeemed by the blood of Jesus Christ, the Savior of us all. And you are saying that He has already made a difference in each of your lives separately, and He will make a difference in your one life together. You are admitting, along with all of us who are Christians, that being human means being full of sin, and sin is the disturber of human relations, including marriage relations. Sin wreaks havoc with human life by causing us to tell lies about relationships to each other and to God—lies that say things are okay when they are not; lies that say things are good as long as they don't hurt anyone; lies that say marriages may last as long as people still can tolerate each other, but there is no need to promise fidelity beyond the time when love ceases; lies that would like to change the marriage commitment from "as long as we both shall live" to "as long as we both shall love."

So, when Christians marry, they tell the truth about sin in us. But they also tell us a cheering and happy and great truth: Jesus has made the difference. His resurrection makes us alive forever.

Because of Him, every Christian marriage can be alive with hope and Christian optimism—the kind of optimism that counters all the horrible statistics of marriage failure and divorce, that shows the sham of all the "how-to" articles in the cheap tabloids at checkout counters, that exposes the tawdriness of the talk-show exposés and the cheap soap operas with their childish intrigue. Christian optimism exposes such evil with the fact that two people and Jesus can make a marriage the most natural, workable, sublime, practical, and lovely union—so lovely that despite the pain and sorrow and hurt that sometimes are there, Christian marriage becomes in the Bible a real example of the relationship that exists between Jesus and the Church.

Therefore, God's Word enjoins us to be "submitting to one another out of reverence for Christ" (Eph 5:21). The Christian husband, by the power of the Holy Spirit, is to endeavor to exercise toward his bride the same unselfish and sacrificial love Jesus demonstrated for His Bride, the Church, when He gave Himself up for her in life and in death. And the bride is to give herself to her husband as the Church gives herself in loving service to her Lord not because she has to or because she is a slave, but because she stands by the grace of God (as does her husband) in that loving and beloved relationship that only comes to those who are one in Christ Jesus. They are born anew in Him through Holy Baptism and, through Word and Sacrament, are continually forgiven and renewed and refreshed. Together with Christ, the Christian husband and wife stand under the primal blessing of creation when, on the sixth day, God stepped back and looked at everything He had made and said, "Behold, it is very good!" And that included marriage.

So, as important as this ceremony itself may be today, it is not nearly as important as the experiences you will have and what you will demonstrate as you continuously forgive and affirm each other, even as Christ does for His Church. Surely you already know that a marriage without quarrels and strife is unreal—an impossible dream and a dangerous delusion. A Christian marriage is one in which both spouses recall what Christ has done for them, recall their vows in the face of differences and pain, and then commit themselves anew to each other with the love that can only come from Christ, who is our Savior and our Lord.

Can you do that? Will you do that? You will, with the help of God. That is possible only with the Holy Spirit. It is only by living in Christ that your lives toward each other will bear that delectable fruit—love, compassion, kindness, and acceptance—that goes beyond just plain tolerance.

None of us knows what lies ahead in that distant country we call the future. But we Christians know that God is there to brighten every morning with His presence and His power for the day and to lighten every night with the brightness of His forgiveness and His peace. With Him, you can do and be all that He intends. Keep near to Him—today and forever.

Rev. John D. Fritz

Yield in Love to God's Design

Ephesians 5:21–33

No mystery meets the eye as we behold you two in anticipatory splendor. Your faces reflect both radiance and reserve as you begin a new relationship that involves "leaving" and "cleaving." You can't comprehend at this moment all the "believing" you will need to make your marriage the spiritual reality that God intends it to be. Begin by being thankful for your relationship rather than by being desirous of its perfection. God will take care of the imperfections. After all, "sin has made us all dysfunctional in relationships. As Christians we confess the sin, accept the forgiveness, and get on with life."[2]

When husbands and wives voluntarily yield themselves in love to one another, they reverence Christ. Physically speaking, they are a unit in God's design, "[the two] shall become one flesh" (Gen 2:24). Personal pride will divide that unity. Spiritually speaking, the Savior must be their mutual means for marriage maintenance. Jesus is the original volunteer and yielder in God's plan of salvation for all people in all relationships, including marriage.

YIELD TO HIS DESIGN

As husband and wife, you two will become one flesh. You will remain the individuals you are as male and female. Yet it is necessary to treat each other as one. Don't let personal pride your unity divide. To haggle over gender issues, for example, based on "superior-inferior" criteria, is not constructive. Because God loves you in Jesus Christ, in Christian marriage you are obligated and privileged to let such sacrificial love lead your life together.

Reverence Christ by voluntarily yielding to your husband in earthly matters. United to him, he will belong to you. Saving faith provides freedom for you to yield to him to the extent you yield to Christ. Take your cue from Paul: "Do not use your freedom as an opportunity for the flesh, but through love serve one another" (Gal 5:13). Anticipate direction from your husband as God's antidote for both of you when chaos clouds the relationship. Yield to him gratefully in light of God's gracious indication: "There is neither Jew nor Greek, there is neither slave nor free, there is neither male nor female, for you are all one in Christ Jesus" (Gal 3:28).

Reverence Christ by voluntarily yielding to your wife in the nooks and crannies of life by loving her as Christ loves the Church. Your assignment is headship, not

---

2 Eldon Weisheit, *Share Life's Defining Moments* (St. Louis: Concordia, 1997), 52

lordship. Your love for her can spare no sacrifice. Love calls for a constant attitude and consistent action from you toward her. Ideally, you should both love and like her. But there will be times when loving must remain because liking won't. It's analogous to God, who hates sin but loves the sinner. Such love springs from respecting your own forgiven personhood. Because you are, in time, inseparably united to her, the way you care for her is a statement about yourself. Anything done disrespectfully toward her indicts you as being self-detrimental.

Together you must reverence Christ by yielding to His order. That arrangement presupposes that every marriage is sovereign, second to none, including those of your immediate families. Although you need to be a legal adult to be married, marriage doesn't always guarantee mature adulthood. Cozy co-dependencies can soon lead to rebellious resentments. You'll grow into adulthood as you accept responsibility for your own marriage. Discuss and use, if applicable, what worked for your parents. What won't, don't. Just be genuinely firm in your own solidarity and the in-laws will less likely become out-laws.

REVERENCE CHRIST

Reverence Christ by voluntarily yielding to His forgiving direction of your marriage. "For God so loved the world, that He gave His only Son, that whoever believes in Him should not perish but have eternal life" (Jn 3:16). Paul reminds us that Jesus, "though He was in the form of God, did not count equality with God a thing to be grasped, but made Himself nothing, taking the form of a servant, being born in the likeness of men. And being found in human form, He humbled Himself by becoming obedient to the point of death, even death on a cross" (Phil 2:6–8).

Your mutual understanding of God's total claim on your individual lives will be demonstrated in your marriage. Because Christ is everything to you, you will treat one another accordingly. You will accept the other as justified and sanctified by God for loving service with you. Since you both are children of God, your marriage may be motivated by God's gracious will, not by fleeting feelings.

Jesus' love is both standard and model for Christian marriage. His love for the Church causes the voluntary yielding of the Church in reverence to Him. Likewise, the husband's for his wife. His self-sacrificing love makes it a delight for his wife to voluntarily yield herself to him. What wife can maintain the voluntary yielding intended by the Lord in marriage without intelligent and purposeful love demonstrated by her husband? And as both husband and wife abide in Christ's Bride, the Church, they can be sustained because Jesus "gave Himself up for her" (Eph 5:25).

Until in glory Jesus gathers His Bride for an eternal feast of victory, we support you both in His amazing grace and abundant mercy so that you might reverence Christ by a voluntary yielding in love to one another throughout your married life.

Rev. William L. Couch

The Martyrdom of Marriage

Colossians 1:27

One of the collects used in the Orthodox Church at a marriage is for martyrdom. Martyrdom is not so far removed from what we observe in this hour—a Christian wedding (a nuptial Eucharist). Each of you is heading into a "martyrdom" of sorts. I do not speak lightly. It is the "martyrdom" of self for the other: the total giving of oneself in marriage, even as Christ "gave Himself," "poured Himself out," for the Church—and for the whole world—in suffering and dying for the sins of humanity on the cross.

Yes, it is from our Lord that we learn the true nature of marriage. Not that we see our Lord Jesus Christ as a mere example of self-giving. We can't emulate Him. We are sinners, and so often we fail to be the "little Christs" to each other that He daily calls us to be. So, we look not on our Lord's martyrdom and self-giving as only a model to follow. Rather, devoid of any power of our own, we ask for His Holy Spirit to do that in us which we are unable to do. As Scripture says, "It is God who works in you, both to will and to work for His good pleasure" (Phil 2:13). As the apostle Paul says in our text and more than thirty times in the New Testament, it "is Christ in you" (Col 1:27).

Being "Christ in you" and "Christ in you" to each other can make your marriage first and foremost, by the central aspect of Christ's work, a place of forgiveness.

A man had made a fool of himself at a party. The next day he felt complete remorse for his actions and begged his wife to forgive him. "I do, honey," she promised.

But over the next few months, whenever something came up that displeased the wife, she would bring up the party incident. "I thought you forgave me for that," the husband said.

"Darling, I did forgive you—I just don't want you to forget that I forgave you," she replied.

God's forgiveness is not like that. When He forgives, He forgets. He says through the prophet Isaiah, "I, I am He who blots out your transgressions for My own sake, and I will not remember your sins" (Is 43:25). Therefore, you and I are called to "forgive and forget" daily. Oh, humanly speaking, we remember what happened. But God calls us to forgive and not keep on holding against the other person the wrong that happened.

So forgiveness is the key to your new relationship of marriage, *(names)*. For we are all imperfect human beings. *(Name)* is always late, and *(name)* is always . . . I am speaking of our self-centered natures. In the intimacy of marriage, our self is always getting in the way. Take a long walk to try to get away from your selfish self; come back, and sitting on the doorstep of your marriage will be your same self.

Therefore, the best of Christian marriages requires constant forgiveness. Each day you and I—all of us here—need to remember that we walk as a man or woman forgiven by God not because we're doing a "pretty good job" in being a faithful Christian, but because God in Christ has absorbed our sinful selfishness into Himself—by His death on the cross.

Christ died for our sins. And as Scripture says, "Therefore welcome one another as Christ has welcomed you" (Rom 15:7). That's the divine design for your marriage: the plan for forgiveness. Not an "easy" forgiveness. Not "to continue in sin that grace may abound" (Rom 6:1). Not "cheap grace." But the "costly grace" of Christ. His holy calling to each of you now is to be a "little Christ" to the other person daily, in thought, in word, and in action.

Three words: "Please forgive me." Not just "I'm sorry." Or "I'm sorry you found out." But "Please forgive me. And, in the name of Christ, I forgive you."

When that happens regularly, then, by the daily memory of your Baptism (which Luther said we are to put on like a garment every morning), the Holy Spirit will cause your love to grow. Not just a love to be loved. And not only a love for the other person. But more: it will be a love that seeks to capture God's vision of what the other person can become. It will be a self-denying love that, by Christ's indwelling, strives to enable the other person to become the individual God wants that person to be. That's exciting and adventurous!

I call you to that love. With that kind of love in mind, you will say to each other: "*(Name)*, I love you more than yesterday, but less than tomorrow." And "*(Name)*, I love you more than yesterday, but less than tomorrow." Amen.

Rev. Donald L. Deffner

Basic Necessities

Colossians 3:12–15

Traveling in northern Canada in early spring when roads were still nearly impassable, a college president came upon this sign: "Take care which rut you choose. You'll be in it for the next twenty-five miles" (source unknown).

It's not my intention to compare marriage to a rut, but someone wiser than I has compared marriage to a journey—a bus trip, to be exact. From all the buses in the world, you board one. That bus could represent the circle of people you know through family and friends, school, and work. Once on board among that group of people, you select one seat, beside one partner. Ever after, your primary business is to remain with that one partner. More people may get on the bus; some may get off. Your bus may have a flat tire or accident or take a detour. You two might even agree to get off and board a different bus traveling toward your shared destination. But whatever the itinerary, the one pledge you must never break is that you will remain beside your partner. Together you will travel the road ahead, sharing life's adventures, bumps, breakdowns, and discoveries, journeying toward the common destination of all Christians: the heavenly city, the new Jerusalem.

You began that journey when you were baptized into Christ. That was arguably the single most important day in your life. While marriage does not change your destination, it is nevertheless a momentous occasion, for now there will be three of you traveling together inseparably, united as one.

We are honored that you have invited us to be here with you at your "bon voyage" celebration as this new leg of your journey begins. You have also invited the apostle Paul to your big day. A wise choice, because he knows a thing or two about significant journeys. In fact, his words—recorded in Holy Scripture—provide a checklist of basic necessities for every couple starting out. What's interesting to notice is that he focuses not so much on the beginning of the journey, such as how we should dress today or what the menu or the entertainment will include at the reception, but on the necessities for the trip—the entire trip. He writes, "Put on then, as God's chosen ones, holy and beloved, compassion, kindness, humility, meekness, and patience, bearing with one another and, if one has a complaint against another, forgiving each other; as the Lord has forgiven you, so you also must forgive. And above all these put on love, which binds everything together in perfect harmony. And let the peace of Christ rule in your hearts, to which indeed you were called in one body. And be thankful."

Paul's idea here is that certain things never go out of style. Basic necessities, we might call them. That's what you want to take with you as you set out. Let's focus on three of them.

God's Coat of Love

The foremost item for every couple starting out is a coat, an all-weather, one-size-fits-all kind of coat. It is available to everyone, everywhere, though you won't find it in the stores. It is prohibitively expensive, though it costs you nothing to acquire it. It is the coat of God's love in Christ. You were clothed with Christ in Baptism (Gal 3:27), which, St. Paul said a little earlier (Col 2:11–13), marks a dying with Christ and a rising to new life with Christ—the start of your Christian life, your journey, as we have pictured it. God's love in Christ cloaks you in His righteousness and outfits you to show appropriate love in all aspects of your life. And there is no more important relationship for the showing of love than marriage.

You may have looked for many desirable qualities in your partner. But one is supreme: "Above all these," Paul writes, "put on love, which binds everything together in perfect harmony" (v. 14).

This coat of love is not just any kind of coat, because this is not just any kind of love. This is a coat of Christian love, not merely an emotion or affection. This love-coat isn't romantic love, either, though that is also precious and valuable. This coat is made of the kind of love that is an act of the will in addition to a pull of the heart. This kind of love begins with God, who has willed to love us, even though we did not deserve it.

In another of his letters Paul explains such outrageous love: "While we were still weak, at the right time Christ died for the ungodly" (Rom 5:6). This is "love to the loveless shown That they might lovely be" (*LSB* 430:1).

Before you were even conceived, God planned for you to have this coat of love. He wrapped you in it the day He claimed you in Holy Baptism and planted faith in Jesus in your heart. He saw to it that this coat would cost you nothing. Jesus paid for this love-coat with the price of His life. Do you see what this means for you? God is always there to wrap you anew in His love, even when you fail and fail miserably. Sin is serious business. We not only feel guilty; we are guilty. But God's coat covers all our sin so that we become a new creation, ready to start out again for home, no matter what shape we were in before.

Today, as you board your bus and take your seat, your calling is to help keep each other bundled up in this coat of love.

Under God you have decided to marry one unique person—the one standing beside you. Marriage now becomes your vocation, your calling. And to what is God calling you? To keep wrapping your partner in this coat of love.

That course of action does not necessarily come automatically or easily. Albert Einstein reportedly once said, "Women marry men hoping they will change, and men marry women hoping they will not. So each is inevitably disappointed." Perhaps such disappointment is why we set about to improve one another! Often our method is to point out every mistake and every fault of our partner. We may even expect perfection of one another, something we can really expect only from God.

Now, our Lord does not ask us to condone wrongdoing. But He does teach us to pray, "Forgive us our trespasses as we forgive those who trespass against us." Sure, each of us has weaknesses and failures, as well as positive abilities and strengths. God calls us married people to focus our thinking on what is good and true. And He calls us to keep the coat of Christian love wrapped around one another, even as He has wrapped us in His perfect love in Christ.

Your Peacemaker

Paul says that there is another basic necessity for every couple starting out. It is a peacemaker. I didn't say a pacemaker, but a peacemaker. "Let the peace of Christ rule in your hearts," Paul continues, "to which indeed you were called in one body" (v. 15).

What, exactly, is this peacemaker we can't do without?

It is peace that is very different from the peace most people experience. That is as Jesus promised. "Peace I leave with you; My peace I give to you. Not as the world gives do I give to you," He says (Jn 14:27).

Many couples today do not look at the prospect of marriage with much peace. Here are some examples that show what happens without the foundation of Christian love and peace. A reporter once asked her readers what they thought were the best words a man and woman could say to each other on their wedding day, if not the traditional and time-honored "I do." Respondents revealed little certainty or hope about marriage as they replied that everything from "I hope so" to "I'll try" seemed more appropriate to the level of commitment or the reality of the day-to-day married state.[3]

Paul says that as baptized children of God, you take along a very different kind of peacemaker: "The peace of Christ," he calls it. This is not to imply that marriage does not require hard work and an ongoing commitment to nurture the relationship. But such work and commitment can be made with confidence in God, rather than apprehension and uncertainty because of our human failings.

Writing from prison more than fifty years ago, Dietrich Bonhoeffer explained that Christians can approach marriage with peace in our hearts by taking responsibility for our vows even as we place our marriage in God's hands. Bonhoeffer continues: "God sealed your 'I will' with His own. He has crowned your assent with His."[4] Thus as a result of your vows before God, and your love for each other, God brings you into the estate of holy matrimony.

---

3 *Detroit News* (May 26, 1996).

God is intentionally involved in what is taking place here today as you start out on the journey of marriage. Let His promise give you peace. Through Christ, the Maker of all families is making you a family today. He will go with you all the way. Let Him continue to rule your hearts and minds. Ask Him to control your anxieties and fears. When you fight, ask Him to help you arrive at peace.

THANKFULNESS

Paul mentions yet a third basic necessity that every couple starting out needs. He says simply, "And be thankful" (v. 15). While the first basic necessity, the love-coat, is a matter of will and decision, and the second, our peacemaker, is a matter of faith, this third basic necessity is a matter of attitude.

In a few moments, you will make promises to each other. You are about to take on a very serious commitment. Your vows remind us that marriage is work.

You are going to promise that you will stay with one another in sickness and health. Let's be honest: most of us are not a joy to be around when we are sick. We are not thoughtful of others. We are not very considerate. Certainly, we aren't very attractive. If this is how we are with a cold, imagine how challenging it will be when there is serious illness. Now, Paul says to take along for such times not just a grin-and-bear-it, grit-your-teeth-and-hang-in-there attitude, but a gratitude attitude. Be thankful for this flu-ridden grouch!

In a few moments you'll also promise that, rich or poor, you're going to stay married. It may be true that two can live as cheaply as one, but not as well! Good-bye creature comforts! Add a few children, and it's "hello, sacrifice." Again, Paul says, go into this with your eyes open and your heart offering thanksgiving. Have a gratitude attitude.

Louis H. Evans, onetime chaplain of the United States Senate, caught the impact of God's higher purposes that find fulfillment through marriage. In a prayer that Evans composed for a bride and groom, he asked, "God of love . . . make such assignments to them as will develop their character as they walk together. Give them enough tears to keep them tender, enough hurts to keep them human, enough failure to keep their hands clenched tightly in thine, and enough success to encourage them in their walk with thee."[5]

Today you embark together on the leg of your "bus trip" that will not end until one or both of you reach the heavenly destination of the journey you began in Baptism. Whatever else, take along these necessities, and make use of them always: God's coat of love; Christ, the peacemaker; and an attitude of gratitude, because God indeed is going with you.

Rev. David V. Koch

---

4 Dietrich Bonhoeffer, *Letters and Papers from Prison*, pp. 149–50.

5 Copyright © American Tract Society, P.O. Box 462008, Garland, TX 75046. www.atstracts.org. Used with permission.

You Must Be Crazy: A Wedding Sermon for Divorced Persons

1 John 4:7

Some people would say, "You must be crazy to want to make marriage promises to each other." Today, you will promise to give yourselves to one another in "heart, body, and mind," totally. It matters not whether "for better or worse, for richer or poorer, in sickness and in health." Today, you will promise "to love and to cherish," to give yourselves to one another "as long as you both shall live." Yes, you must be crazy—crazy in love.

In fact, no couple who has made these promises, not one, has always kept them. No wife has always respected and esteemed her husband. No husband has always loved and cherished his bride. No marriage yet has been free from sin and selfishness.

Each of you has lived through the pain of divorce. Promises made were broken. Yet now you want to make these vows again. You must be crazy. You must be crazy in love.

(Name) and *(name)*, if this is crazy, then God is the master of crazy love. Think how crazy His love was at the cross—full and free forgiveness for all our faults. You can stake His life on it. Crazy love. His love is as crazy as Easter. Love even stronger than the grave that rises up to give new life and a new start, fresh and clean.

Crazy love. Love so wild and wonderful that He promises: "*(Name)* and *(name)*, I join you together. By My love, My forgiveness, I have made just the man for *(name)*. By My love, My forgiveness, I have made just the right woman for *(name)*. I have brought you to this day. By My love, My forgiveness, let your marriage thrive. Let your love take wing and fly."

The pastor does not invent this. Jesus promises, "The man will be united to his wife, and the two will become one flesh. So you are no longer two, but one flesh. You two, God has joined together" (cf. Mt 19:5–6). Jesus has endless love, endless forgiveness, for you in your marriage. Jesus will never fail you. Why? He is crazy in love with you.

With all the love in your hearts, make your promises gladly. It is not crazy to believe that Jesus gives you this love to share. It is not crazy to believe that Jesus will give you even more love in the years ahead.

Rev. Stephen E. Gaulke

O Perfect Love

1 John 4:7–12

A number of years ago there was a television commercial in which a man ran back and forth in a parking lot full of bright yellow trucks. As he ran from one truck to another, he said, "Ryder rents trucks. Ryder rents big trucks. Ryder rents small trucks. Ryder rents pickup trucks. Ryder rents moving trucks. Ryder rents dump trucks. Ryder rents vans." Then he asked, "Now what did I say?" It was hard to miss the point.

BY THE NUMBERS

The apostle John may well have asked the same question at the end of our text: "Now what did I say?" His message, however, is not about trucks, but about love. John uses the word *love* thirteen times in the space of the six verses of our text, twenty-seven times in the space of this section of his Epistle, and forty-six times in the five chapters of the entire Epistle. This is the same John who identifies himself as the disciple whom Jesus loved, the disciple who was Spirit-inspired to record, "For God so loved the world, that He gave His only Son, that whoever believes in Him should not perish but have eternal life" (Jn 3:16). Now what did I say? The message is love—God's love for us and our love for one another.

Love has brought you together and love will keep you together. John calls us—husbands and wives, parents and children, brothers and sisters, family and friends—to love one another in the style and strength of our Lord Jesus Christ. We love because He first loved us.

THE VERY FIRST MARRIAGE

God's plan for His people—and for marriage—was established at the very beginning. God created Adam and Eve in His own image—not physically, but with a spiritual nature. Adam and Eve were to reflect God's nature to one another. That's why God said later, "Don't make any graven images of Me because you are My image." Thus when Adam and Eve went about their daily tasks, as they spoke and listened and touched one another, they knew that their relationship was holy and special, ordained of God. Each saw God in the other, for each had been created in the image of God.

How long did that perfection last? Nobody knows, but let's stop for a moment and savor the splendor, for that is nearly as close to heaven on earth as possible.

We know, however, what follows: the fruit tree and the serpent and sin. And with that everything changed. Now when Eve looked at Adam, she saw Adam. And when Adam looked at Eve, he saw Eve. No longer was God uppermost in their lives. No longer did they reflect the image of God and act out God's will. Now Adam was primarily concerned about Adam, and Eve was primarily concerned about Eve.

Placing the Blame Where It Belongs

How convenient it would be for us to point the finger of blame at Adam and Eve and say, "It's all your fault. If you had not succumbed to the serpent, everything would be different today. We would still be enjoying things the way God meant them to be." Adam and Eve were acting not only on their own behalf but also on behalf of all humanity. Their names could just as easily have been John and Mary or Ted and Alice or *(name)* and *(name)*. We show that we are children of Adam and Eve by playing the same blame game and keeping score with one another. The result is that everybody gets hurt.

Jesus Is God's Perfect Image

Imagine God's disappointment and anger with Adam and Eve. He would have been justified in destroying them and making a fresh start. Actually, He did in the life of Jesus Christ, a plan that was in place already before the dawn of creation. Fast-forward several thousand years to a stable in Bethlehem, where Jesus was born as the perfect image of God. In Jesus Christ, God was making a fresh start. Jesus was the second Adam, the perfect Adam. Jesus was the second Eve, the perfect Eve. Where Adam and Eve failed, Jesus succeeded. Jesus was the person God created Adam and Eve to be. He is the person God has created you and me to be. Jesus obeyed perfectly God's commandment to love, and God credits that obedience to our account. Jesus paid in full the penalty for our scorekeeping and our finger-pointing by dying on the cross, and God declares us forgiven, beloved children, sons and daughters of God. The evangelist John describes that love in this way: "God so loved the world, that He gave His only Son" for me, for you. You are loved. You are forgiven.

You are beautiful in the eyes of God. Now you are called to love one another because God first loved us.

Disagreements Happen

Somebody has said that if there are never any disagreements in marriage, one of the two partners is unnecessary. This is simply a way of saying, "It happens; it goes with the territory." Disagreements are real. It is not a matter of if, but when, and then what? What do you do when there are disagreements? Talk and listen. Listen and talk. And then talk some more and listen some more. A fellow pastor and friend used to wear two buttons on the lapels of his coat. One said, "You may be right; let's talk." The other one said, "I may be wrong; let's talk." The talking and listening may lead to "I'm sorry" and "I forgive you." When the lines of communication remain open, the potential for misunderstanding is lessened and the possibility for growth increases. We can talk and we can listen and we can confess and we can forgive because we are loved by God with a perfect love.

Perfect Love

Our love at best is always an imperfect love, but when it is offered in the spirit of Christ, it becomes a beautiful expression. Those are the moments when we look at another person and say, "You know, you remind me of somebody." And that somebody is Jesus, who is living in and loving through that other person. Neither of us may be beautiful as the world perceives beauty. But our Lord's love for us and our love for each other are a beauty to behold. That's a glimpse of glory, a small slice of the way it was with Adam and Eve in the Garden of Eden, the way it will be when all things are made new and perfect in heaven.

One of the best gifts that one person can give to another person is his or her love—willingly, joyfully, no strings attached. And one of the best gifts that the other person can give is to receive that gift of love—willingly, joyfully. We can give love and receive love because we are loved. God loved us first, last, and always.

Rev. Paul T. Prange

Civil Holidays

New Year's Day

The Year under the Cross
Philippians 2:9–13

New Year's Day has become a national holiday here in the United States, but it is not, strictly speaking, a part of our church calendar. The reason for this is obvious: when we remember that the Christian Church is found throughout the world, then we are faced with the following questions: which secular calendar shall we observe? Which New Year's Day? How about the Chinese new year? Or we could pick one of three or four calendars that are found within the pages of Scripture. Or we could pick one of the several calendars with which we ourselves operate, such as the tax year, which ends on April 15, or perhaps the fiscal year, which often begins on July 1.

Needless to say, the calendar that is most pertinent to the life of the Church is the liturgical calendar. The Church marks her time and gears her life according to Christ and what He has done, not by what we happen to be doing. According to this calendar, which began on November 29 *(change date as necessary)*, the First Sunday in Advent, today we remember the circumcision of our Savior as a 1-week-old infant. It is also a day to remember the name that He received on that occasion: the name *Jesus*, "the Lord saves," the name that crowns all of *(year)*.

The apostle Paul wanted the Church at Philippi to know the significance of the name *Jesus* for her day-by-day life of faith. This congregation was near and dear to Paul's heart, and the feeling was mutual. The Philippian Church was the first congregation that Paul started on the European continent. They loved Paul very dearly and showed their love by lending him support during his imprisonment in Rome. What was troubling Paul was that this congregation was having a hard time. It was very small; despite its overflowing generosity toward other Christians in need, it was very poor; and, most important, it was suffering persecution at the hands of both the Romans and the Jews. To these people laboring under such hard times Paul gives the only rock-solid comfort he could ever offer. He tells them again of the name *Jesus*, which includes everything that Christ is, has done, and will do for them. Paul does so by quoting what may have been an ancient Christian hymn, a hymn that calls to mind those words of the prophet Isaiah:

> Turn to Me and be saved, all the ends of the earth! For I am God, and there is no other. By Myself I have sworn; from My mouth has gone out in righ-

teousness a word that shall not return: "To Me every knee shall bow, every tongue shall swear allegiance." (Is 45:22–23)

But the suffering of the Philippian believers is not the heart of the matter. The question we must be asking is, How can the twenty-first-century Church endure troublesome times? How can the Church in your house deal with hard times? The answer is not only can the Church endure hard times, but we can also find our true glory in these times. Yes, we can even rejoice in those times with a joy that will not fade away no matter how hard those times become. Such joy is in the name *Jesus* and what it signifies. The answer is to be found in that precise moment when Jesus is truly being Jesus in the fullest sense of the term. Most specifically, the answer is to be found in the cross of our Lord Jesus Christ.

Here is the way Paul puts it. Why has the Father in heaven exalted His Son to the highest place of all? Why shall all creatures bow at the name of Jesus? Why shall every tongue confess Jesus as Lord of all and give glory to God the Father? Because Jesus did not use His equality with God to escape suffering. Instead, He made Himself nothing, took the very nature of a servant, was made in human likeness, and humbled Himself. Yes, He was being obedient to death, no more and no less than His death on the cross!

To the Lord Jesus Himself the cross always was and always shall be His most glorious moment. It was His "hour," His moment of truth, His hour of glory that no one could rob Him of. When He was lifted up on the cross, He was "lifted up," that is, exalted above every other name in heaven and earth and under the earth. The cross marked His victory over sin, death, hell, and Satan. To this day God is reigning from the tree with "rich wounds, yet visible above, In beauty glorified" (*LSB* 525:3). The glory of Jesus is the moment when the work of redemption and eternal salvation is complete, and He shouts, "It is finished!" It was on the cross that Jesus, "the Lord saves," lived up to His wonderful name-above-all-names as He drew all people to Himself.

Now, when Jesus says that the cross is His most glorious moment, make no mistake about it, He really means it. He is not looking at His entire self-sacrificing work for us through some kind of rose-colored glasses, as though He claims it is His glory but in fact He knows better. In all His Jesus-work for our sakes, He was not temporarily stepping outside His true self, becoming someone He was not, all the while longing for the time when He could become His true self once again. The cross really is His glory. It is the pure reflection of His true character. On Mount Sinai, God revealed to Moses that His true glory is His goodness and mercy. The glory of His Son, Jesus, is the same goodness and mercy, which can be summed up in two words: the cross.

Nor does the resurrection of the Lord Jesus diminish the glory of Jesus' victory on the cross! It was not, as one church billboard once announced, "The Uncrucifixion of Jesus." The resurrection testifies to the fact that the victory won at the cross was a real victory. The empty tomb shows us that each blessing won at the cross—every last one of them—has already started to flow to you and me.

With all these things in mind, the apostle Paul then turns his attention to the Philippians and to us. What about us? What about the hardships we will have to face in *(year)*? In the verses immediately surrounding our text, Paul issues statements that make sense to us only when we view them in light of the cross. Just before our text he says, "Let your manner of life be worthy of the gospel of Christ. . . . For it has been granted to you that for the sake of Christ you should not only believe in Him but also suffer for His sake, engaged in the same conflict that you saw I had and now hear that I still have" (1:27, 29–30). Shortly after our text Paul says, "Even if I am to be poured out as a drink offering upon the sacrificial offering of your faith, I am glad and rejoice with you all. Likewise you also should be glad and rejoice with me" (2:17–18). And "Have this mind among yourselves, which is yours in Christ Jesus" (2:5).

By now the words of Paul should be crystal clear. As people who bear the name of Jesus, as people who have received through the cross all the blessings we could ever possibly need and desire for time and eternity, as people who have been baptized into His death and resurrection, we have become new people. As we take up our cross and follow Him, the cross is our glory too. In the cross of Christ I glory. It is not as though the life of service and sacrifice we lead in the name of Jesus were our glory; it really is our glory. We count it all as joy when we face various trials, because it really is our joy. Through the blood of the cross, we have already stepped outside of our old selves as lost and condemned sinners, and we have become a new forgiven people with the mind-set and purpose of Jesus in our hearts.

What then shall we say about *(year)*? Again, Paul says it best in the text (vv. 12–13): "Work out your own salvation with fear and trembling, for it is God who works in you, both to will and to work for His good pleasure."

As baptized children of God, we already see emblazoned over the entire year the name above all names, the name of Jesus, our Savior. In the new year we may not have to face times that were as tough as the Philippians faced. Then again, we may. But regardless of what happens, since you have been crucified and raised to new life with Christ, each and every day will be an occasion for joy. That is a promise from the very one who bears the name *Jesus* to those who bear the same name.

In this new year things will happen that will lead our weak flesh to worry. Indeed, events will cause us to tremble with fear, but, by God's grace, we will make it through them all. Even when we suffer for righteousness' sake, we will count it all joy. In all our sufferings we are only being true to our new selves re-created in the image of the Lord Jesus. Every pain we experience is nothing less than a participation in the cross of Jesus, the very cross that means life for us. Every pain we endure is a reminder of all the blessings Jesus has won for us. In short, life under the cross is a wonderful, glorious thing.

How do you, to use Paul's words, "continue to work out your salvation?" By clinging to the cross, where Jesus has worked it all out for us. The fear and trembling come precisely at the moment we again realize that we can "work out" nothing by ourselves. But the trembling stops and gives way to perfect calm at the foot of the cross. There at the cross we look up and see the one named *Jesus*, "My Savior, my Savior!" We see the one who will always be His true self—always. Look at the blood, the tears, the agony. Never has the world seen such compassion, such forgiveness, such glory.

More pointedly, we return regularly to the foot of the cross as we adhere to "the word of life" (v. 16). Every time we return to that Word in *(year)* we shall be reminded of our true glory: His cross and our life under His cross. Every time we turn to that Word with fear and trembling, we shall receive true peace in knowing that God is working out His good pleasure in us. And we shall be directly linked to that cross as we receive the very body and blood of our Lord in His Supper.

(Year) will be for us the "year of the cross." For us in this place, it will be a rejoicing in death—the death of Jesus, the Savior. Just as we participate in Jesus' death, we shall also participate in His resurrection. In tears and in laughter the joy never ends. In Jesus, our joy is as lasting as His glory:

> The death of Jesus Christ, our Lord
> We celebrate with one accord. (*LSB* 634:1)

Rev. James G. Bollhagen

Life Sunday

Jesus Loves Children

Mark 10:13–16

Jesus loves children. The crowds of people who were following Him at this particular time sensed this. There was something about this teacher, something about the things He said, something about His hands, His touch. They had seen those hands touch and heal many in the crowd. So they brought their children. Luke's account uses a word indicating many were babies. They brought these little ones just hoping Jesus would touch them. Jesus loves children. They could just tell.

TWO OPPOSING VIEWS

But the disciples said hands-off to these baby-bringers. Jesus shouldn't be bothered with little children. He had more important things to do. He had to preach and teach and heal. The disciples were not polite. They actually "rebuked" (v. 13) those who tried to have Jesus touch their babies. Jesus loves children? Well, as far as the disciples were concerned, He had better things to do.

Jesus loves children? There seem to be two opposing views in our text. It's hard to imagine—or is it? We live in a country that loves children. We have people and places and programs dedicated solely to helping children. When children die, as in the Oklahoma City bombing years ago, sadness and mourning grip the entire nation. The death of children makes tragic news even more tragic. How often we read this kind of headline: "Ten Die in Fire—Six of Them Children." Death is hard to accept. The death of children is unacceptable.

At the same time, we live in a country where many, even in the Church, favor abortion or defend it as a right. But no matter how much verbal engineering we do by calling it a "right" or a "choice" or the "termination of a pregnancy," it is the death of a child. There are not many informed people, even those who are pro-choice, who deny that anymore. Yet our country's love for children does not seem to extend to those in the womb. We don't see the tragedy if the headlines read, "Four Thousand Abortions Performed Today—Four Thousand Children Die."

Jesus loves children. The people sensed it; the disciples tried to deny it. Jesus, however, demonstrates it. In the remainder of our text He does two things to His disciples. He rebukes and He teaches. Then He does three things to the children. He reaches, touches, and blesses. Let's look briefly at each of these in an effort to understand the scope of Jesus' love for children.

Jesus Rebukes

First, Jesus does some rebuking of His own. His rebuke is strong. He is "indignant" (v. 14) over the attitude of the disciples. In today's vernacular, He's "ticked off" at their "hands-off" attitude. We can understand the way Jesus reacted. What would you do if every Sunday morning, twelve leaders of the congregation did their best to keep children from coming to Sunday School? We would be indignant at this absurd action. Why would anyone choose to hinder someone else from learning about Jesus and His love? But isn't that what abortion does in the name of choice? It hinders children from being brought to Jesus. Yet this choice is supported by many in the Church, even by many leaders in the Church. Where is the indignation?

When those in the Church refuse to address abortion because it is "political" or "divisive," they hinder others from learning about Jesus' love as well. Those in a crisis pregnancy situation or those struggling with guilt in the aftermath of an abortion may never hear of Jesus' love and forgiveness and healing applied to their sin. That is one reason why many who find themselves in these situations feel they have committed an unforgivable sin. Why would anyone want to hinder someone else from learning of Jesus' love for them? That is what is happening in many of our churches today. Where is the indignation?

Jesus Teaches

Jesus, however, does not only rebuke His disciples. He also teaches. The children become object lessons of what it takes to enter the kingdom of God. The kingdom of God belongs to those who receive it "like a child" (v. 15). Jesus is not talking about the innocence of children. That would contradict God's Word: "Behold, I was brought forth in iniquity, and in sin did my mother conceive me" (Ps 51:5). Jesus is talking about the smallness of children, about their lack of wisdom to make appropriate decisions on their own, and their need to be totally reliant on someone else. That is how we are to be. We are to deny our "bigness" and confess our "smallness." Remember what Jesus did when the disciples were having one of their frequent discussions about who was the greatest? "Calling to Him a child, He put him in the midst of them." Then Jesus said, "Whoever humbles himself like this child is the greatest in the kingdom of heaven" (Mt 18:2, 4).

As we listen to Jesus teach, we realize that this scene is more than some "cute" event involving children. It is a picture of Jesus' relationship with us. Jesus loves children, and all who receive Him are His children! It is when we forget we are His children that we fall into the trap of relying on ourselves and thinking we have the wisdom to make choices only God can make. We try to make ourselves bigger than God. We make decisions about who should live and who should die—

whether they be God's children in the womb or God's children in the nursing home or God's children suffering from a terminal disease. We behave as if God does not love His children. But God does love children, and the rest of our text gives us a picture of how much He loves them. He reaches and touches and blesses.

JESUS REACHES OUT HIS ARMS

Jesus loves children. In our text Jesus reaches out and takes these children in His arms. This is no superficial pat on the head. Jesus initiates a personal relationship with these children. He reaches out to all helpless individuals and takes them into His arms. They are not just any arms either! Scripture has some things to say about these arms. They are loving arms. "He will tend His flock like a shepherd; He will gather the lambs in His arms" (Is 40:11). They are powerful arms. The psalmist writes, "You have a mighty arm; strong is Your hand" (Ps 89:13).

Are you a teen struggling with tough decisions? Do you find yourself in a crisis pregnancy situation? Do you or does someone you love have a terminal disease? Are you faced with end-of-life decisions for an aging parent? Is there an ache in your heart because of a past abortion, a miscarriage, or some other loss? As you picture these little children, these babies, in Jesus' arms, picture yourself there. There is nothing too difficult for those loving and powerful arms. They reach out to those who are hurting and in need of help.

HIS HANDS ARE GOD'S HANDS

Jesus loves children. In our text, He puts His hands on them and touches them. As the people there sensed, these are not just any hands. These were the hands of God, hands that created the universe and everything in it. These are the hands that created life out of the dust of the ground. These are the hands that continue to create life, knitting us together in our mother's womb. Isaiah pictures these hands as the hands of a potter. "But now, O LORD, You are our Father; we are the clay, and You are our potter; we are all the work of Your hand" (Is 64:8).

These hands willingly stretched out and were nailed to a cross. He, the Holy Child of God, took the place of all the children of God. "Since therefore the children share in flesh and blood, He Himself likewise partook of the same things, that through death He might destroy the one who has the power of death, that is, the devil" (Heb 2:14). The punishment of our sin fell upon Him, and His holiness was given to us. We who are by nature children of wrath are reborn as forgiven children of God through faith in Jesus' pierced hands. Because of the blood they shed on our behalf, those hands have forgiven our sins.

Are you a young person who has made a stupid mistake, a regretful decision? Are you dealing with the hurt and regrets of an out-of-wedlock pregnancy? Are you burdened by a past abortion or some other sin that just seems too big to be forgiven? Are you feeling guilty over an end-of-life decision you made? As you picture these children, these babies, being touched by Jesus, picture yourself there. The touch of the nail-scarred hands of our now resurrected Jesus brings forgiveness, not just an overlooking of past sins, but a complete cleansing, a new start.

Rev. James I. Lamb

Graduation

The Changing of the Guard

John 2:1–11

Stand behind the police barricades with me outside Windsor Castle in London, England. Crowds gather here daily to witness the changing of the guard. It is a majestic event, colorful, exciting! Cameras are going off everywhere. *(Take several flash pictures of the congregation from the pulpit.)* There is an air of royalty. One set of guards is replaced by a new set at the entrance to the historic Windsor Castle.

During this graduation service *(ceremony)*, we, too, will experience a changing of the guard.

(There may be some teachers retiring at the end of this academic year whom you would want to recognize at this time. You may announce their replacements. Truly, that would be a changing of the guard.)

You students for the last eight *(four)* years have been serving at your station in life here at this institution of learning, *(name of school)*. You have been recruits, cadets, or sentinels in the process of learning. But now it is time to have a changing of the guard. You will be relinquishing your places, and others will be your replacements. There will be new members to take your place in the choir, as class officers, on the basketball team, as cheerleaders, and so on.

This is not the first time a changing of the guard has taken place for you. Every year when you have moved from one class to another, you have moved on and others have taken your places. You will continue to be involved in a changing of the guard many times in your life: when you leave home, if and when you marry, when you begin or when you leave a job, when you die and leave this world to enter heaven.

Whenever there is a changing of the guard, you are being relieved of one responsibility and are assuming another.

This reminds me of what happened in our Lord's life. Numerous times there was a changing of the guard.

One of the biggest changes came when the very Son of God left the mansions of heaven, became flesh of our flesh, and entered a human family when He was conceived by the power of the Holy Spirit and was born to the Virgin Mary, who was pledged to marry Joseph (Mt 1:18–25).

There was a changing of the guard when Jesus was moved from His birthplace in the stable in Bethlehem to a house, where He lived out His first weeks and months of life. This allowed time for the Wise Men to come and worship Him and offer Him their finest gifts (Mt 2:1–12).

There was a changing of the guard when the fury of King Herod went ballistic. Joseph was warned in a dream to take the young Child and His mother and flee to Egypt (Mt 2:13–18).

There was another changing of the guard when Herod died. The angel of the Lord gave the signal that it was all right to return to the land of Israel (Mt 2:19–20).

There was a changing of the guard when the angel told Joseph not to return to Bethlehem, where Archelaus was ruling in place of his father, Herod. Nazareth in Galilee would be the place to raise the Child in fulfillment of prophecy (Mt 2:21–23). And when Jesus made the transition into His public ministry, He chose as the setting for His first miraculous sign a wedding festival where He changed water into wine. *(Read Jn 2:1–11 in a translation or summarize it in words that relate well to the age group being graduated.)*

Talk about a changing of the guard! Here we have it—Jesus was changing water into wine! He was also changing a bad situation into something good. He was changing anxiety into joy. But He was also changing God's covenant with His people, represented by the six stone water jars standing there for the purification of the Jews. Jesus was about to fulfill the just requirements of the Law and the ancient promises of a Savior who would inaugurate an age of bounteous divine grace; new wine would flow from the hills throughout the land (cf. Amos 9:13–15).

The stone tablets inscribed with the old covenant gave way to the new covenant inscribed in our hearts by the power of the Holy Spirit, so that we have treasure in earthen vessels—our clay jars (2 Cor 4:7). The Old Testament purification rites with water have been replaced by the new covenant with Holy Baptism, the washing of rebirth that cleanses from guilt and grants new life. The new wine of the new covenant comes to us in the Lord's Supper, where we drink the true blood of Christ shed for the forgiveness of sins.

It's as if I took all your report cards for all the years you have been in school, no matter what grades may be on them—A's, B's, C's, D's, or even F's—and changed them all to straight A's. *(Hold up a report card.)* In Christ we are graded as if we had kept every single one of the required laws of God. Oh, it isn't that I have kept God's laws. I have violated the Law as a whole by failing to fulfill all its stipulations and by outright transgressions too. Just ask these teachers if their students have ever broken any of the rules of their classroom or of this school. Just ask these students if they ever had to stay after class or got knocked down a grade or had to do extra assignments. But Jesus has changed the result of all our misdeeds. He has changed our guilt into His innocence.

Don't be afraid of change. Instead, face it with confidence in Christ, who can change water into wine. We are here today to join with you in celebrating the changing of the guard and in seeking God's gracious guidance through the many changes in your life that lie ahead.

—*Rev. Jerrold L. Nichols*

Father's Day

Father, Who's Following You?

Deuteronomy 6:5–9, 20–25; Proverbs 22:6; Ephesians 6:4

Great ships cruise offshore from the southernmost tip of the great nation of Norway to its northernmost coastlands. The ships are not only the pride of the country, but they also bind it together commercially. When a ship goes down, the entire nation watches in stunned silence.

A large vessel did go down in a fjord one night. But those listening to the radio were shocked to hear that a smaller vessel sank soon afterward in exactly the same spot! Everyone wondered how such a strange coincidence could take place. Upon investigation, it was learned that the smaller vessel had not been using its navigational gear. It simply followed the larger ship, thinking nothing could happen to it.[6]

ARE YOU A FATHER?
FATHER, WHO'S BEEN FOLLOWING YOU?

It's a grave responsibility to be a Christian father. Martin Luther noted this when he began his Small Catechism with the words, "As the head of the family should teach [the Christian truths] in a simple way to his household."[7] Any instruction done by others—the teachers in the Lutheran day school, the pastor, the Sunday School teacher, and so on—is done *in loco parentis*—"in the place of the parent."

The Scriptures have much to say about fathers, but the biblical implications of being a Christian father apply also to parents, to mothers, and to grandparents. They apply to older brothers and sisters whose little brothers and sisters look up to them. They apply to all who are being watched, to all who have someone following them: leaders, teachers, managers in business, and all who exercise any kind of authority. In fact, it probably is safe to say that whatever your situation in life—mother, father, single person—someone is following you!

Listen to what God's Word tells us in Deut 6:5: "You shall love the LORD your God with all your heart and with all your soul and with all your might." Our

---

6 Richard Andersen and Donald Deffner, *For Example* (St. Louis: Concordia, 1977), 84–85.

7 *Luther's Small Catechism*, p. 11.

lives are to be focused on God—not on ourselves. That's our basic problem. We're looking in the wrong direction!

The obligation we have to turn ourselves—and those following us—in the right direction is ongoing. God continues in Deuteronomy: "These words that I command you today shall be on your heart. You shall teach them diligently to your children, and shall talk of them when you sit in your house, and when you walk by the way, and when you lie down, and when you rise" (vv. 6–7).

God doesn't mean you should just set aside one hour as so-called "quality time" with a child, and the rest of the time someone else or no one need be in charge. That leads to the situation where a little girl said to her father, "Daddy, may I make an appointment to play with you on Wednesday?"

Deut 6:8–9 stresses our need to follow the commandments of the Lord: "You shall bind them as a sign on your hand, and they shall be as frontlets between your eyes. You shall write them on the doorposts of your house and on your gates." Down to the present day Jewish people have literally done that with phylacteries to tie on their arms and foreheads in prayer and mezuzoth to attach to their doorframes.

God here probably is using metaphorical language that is not to be understood literally, but it is to be understood spiritually—and followed. The point is that our faith is a visual matter. What visible symbols do you have in your home? a cross? a picture of Christ? your child's baptismal banner? other Christian art? maybe even a prayer niche with a votive shelf and a kneeler?

In the New Testament the first churches were house-churches that gathered in the homes of members. A seminarian told me that his 4-year-old boy once walked into a friend's home and said, "Oh, Daddy, this is a church house, just like ours!"

Is Yours a "Church House"?

A foreign student had been in the home of a Christian girlfriend over Christmas vacation. Before this international student was to return home, the mother of her girlfriend asked her if she had enjoyed her stay in their home. To this the young lady, not a Christian, replied, "Yes, I enjoyed my stay very much. But one thing puzzles me. You do not have a God-shelf in your home. In my country everybody has a God-shelf in their house. Do you worship your God only in church?"

That is an incisive question! Many Christians have few visible reminders in their homes of the Christian faith, our Lord and Savior, and His cross.[8]

---

8   Andersen and Deffner, *For Example*, 216.

This training of our children is ongoing, as emphasized in Deut 6:20–25. The father is to remind his children repeatedly of the mighty acts of God. That is what we do as we recount His blessings to us today.

So the scriptural injunctions are clear. These commands and promises from Deuteronomy are summarized in Prov 22:6: "Train up a child in the way he should go; even when he is old he will not depart from it." And in Eph 6:4: "Fathers, do not provoke your children to anger, but bring them up in the discipline and instruction of the Lord."

Christian fathers, we need to be reminded again and again of the grave responsibility we have! There was a sixth-grade girl who brought home an assignment asking her to make detailed comments on two chapters of Scripture. It took her father two hours to help her, but this assignment vividly reminded him again that he was ultimately responsible for her Christian training.

Do you spend time in the Christian training of your child? One parent did not. She was wealthy and hated being tied down to her chronically ill 16-year-old daughter. So she traveled overseas frequently. One day the daughter received from her mother a beautiful Italian vase. The nurse, handing it to her, noted how thoughtful the mother had been to make sure it arrived right on her daughter's birthday.

But the girl ignored the vase and said, "Take it away, take it away! O Mother, Mother, do not send me anything more. No books, no flowers, no vases, no pictures. Send me no more. I want you, you!"

God says to us fathers, "I want you. Not just promises. Not just things. But you." "My son, give Me your heart" (Prov 23:26). And your child wants you. Not just promises. Not just things. But you.

"All your heart" means being a father with all your heart. It means bringing your child up as a Christian. It means keeping the promise you made at Holy Baptism that your child will be brought up in the true knowledge and worship of God, be taught the Ten Commandments, the Creed, and the Lord's Prayer. It means that you place in your child's hands the Holy Scriptures. It means that you bring your child to church faithfully, and at the appropriate age, to the Lord's Table regularly. In all this you point your child "to Jesus, the founder and perfecter of our faith" (Heb 12:2), who suffered and died on the cross for our sins and who rose again, assuring us of eternal life through faith in Him.

It means you as a father will exemplify all those truths. And doing so means spending time with your child.

A boy ran away from home and headed for a large city. He left a note saying he had appreciated the presents his parents had given him over the years, but what he really wanted was for them to listen to him. They were always "too busy." He concluded: "If anybody asks you where I am, tell them I've gone looking for some-body with time, because I've got a lot of things I want to talk about."

Do you take time to talk and listen to your child? Do you raise your child as if nothing else is more important than that child's spiritual future?

You and I often fail in our obligations as fathers, as parents, as grandparents, as older brothers and sisters, as people in positions of leadership and authority. For that we need to repent, to turn, to change.

The Good News is that God does forgive. His gracious mercy also helps you be the loving parent He has called you to be.

He Himself is our Father. Listen to Luther's explanation of the First Article of the Apostles' Creed, as you are to "teach it in a simple way to [your] household":

I believe in God, the Father Almighty, Maker of heaven and earth.

What does this mean? I believe that God has made me and all creatures; that He has given me my body and soul, eyes, ears, and all my members, my reason and all my senses, and still takes care of them.

He also gives me clothing and shoes, food and drink, house and home, wife and children, land, animals, and all I have. He richly and daily provides me with all that I need to support this body and life.

He defends me against all danger and guards and protects me from all evil. All this He does only out of fatherly, divine goodness and mercy, without any merit or worthiness in me. For all this it is my duty to thank and praise, serve and obey Him.

This is most certainly true.[9]

All this our heavenly Father has done—and still does for us! Most important of all, He gave His own Son into death on the cross. There Christ paid for all our failures as a father, as a parent, as an example of the Christian life to those who observe us and follow us. He forgives us just as surely as Christ is risen from the dead. God gives us who have been baptized into Christ the will and the power—the mind of Christ and the resurrection life of Christ—to be what He wants us to be for the sake of all those who follow us.

Rev. Donald L. Deffner

---

9   *Luther's Small Catechism*, pp. 15–16.

Father's Day

He Is Worthy

Luke 7:1–10

"He is worthy" (Lk 7:4). That is what the elders of the Jews said to Jesus about the centurion who had a dear and very sick servant. "He is worthy." He is worthy because though he is a Roman and is in charge of the Romans around Capernaum, he loves the nation of Israel and has built their synagogue, their meeting place. They apparently put good pressure on Jesus to do what this man was asking—heal his dear and ill servant. It is always encouraging to me that Jesus is receptive to such positive, faith-based pressure.

The centurion was "asking Him to come and heal his servant" (v. 3). And when he heard that Jesus was indeed coming, he was overwhelmed. Those elders of the Jews may have thought that he was worthy, but compared to this Jesus, this soldier was overcome with his own sense of unworthiness. He sent friends to stop Jesus from coming. "I am not worth Your coming. I know that they think I am worthy because while I am under orders, I also can give orders. But compared to You, I am very unworthy."

I wonder what the centurion had in mind. Was he recalling some teenage behavior? Was he reflecting on his behavior from the previous week? Was he reviewing some of what had been in his mind and his fantasies? Was he remembering his evil motivation for doing some of the good for which he was getting credit? What happened?

The Jewish leaders said, "He is worthy." The centurion said, "I am unworthy to have You come to my house. I am unworthy to have You heal my servant. You heal the sick. You cure the leper. You cast out evil demons. You are able to speak truth with great power. No, I am unworthy."

And Jesus said, "Not even in Israel have I found such faith" (v. 9). He never even met the centurion. But when the centurion's friends returned to the centurion's house, they found the servant well. Despite the centurion's sense of unworthiness, Christ healed the one whom he loved.

THE GRACE OF GOD PROVIDES HEALING

A lot of men among us know that grace today. On this Father's Day, many people may be saying, "He is a good man. He has done a lot of good. He loves our nation.

He provides for us. He is the world's greatest dad. He is wonderful. He is worthy of our praise and affection."

But I suspect many of us fathers are saying, compared to the One who casts out demons, who heals the lepers, who heals paralytics, and who speaks the word of truth with great authority, we are unworthy. Oh, we can say to some "Go," and they go, to others "Come," and they come, and to some "Do this," and they do it. But we know ourselves. We know some of the sins of our youth, we know what goes through our minds, we know our insensitivities, our self-centeredness, our shortness of patience. We know. We know we are unworthy.

Still, this Jesus heals us. Even when we feel we are unworthy to come into His presence, He heals us—He does our bidding. This is the grace that Jesus, the Son of God, gives to us. In the midst of our unworthiness, He comes to assure us of His love, His forgiveness, His renewing power.

THE WORTHY CHRIST
BECOMES UNWORTHY IN OUR PLACE

In one powerful sense Jesus becomes unworthy, suffering death on the cross reserved for the most unworthy of all, so that we who are so unworthy and deserve such a fate, may be declared worthy before the throne of God.

This is the great Gospel. It is the only Gospel. It is the great Gospel for us. There is no other one. There is no other Gospel than the Gospel that Jesus Christ, God's Son, is the only one who can declare us worthy, and He did that by His innocent suffering, death, and resurrection.

That message is not only for us Christian fathers who gather in a church on Father's Day. It is a message for all of those who are fathers and who have not taken their tasks of fatherhood seriously or with a sense of commitment, for those who have no one who today is saying, "You are the greatest," who have failed in every way in their fathering.

Hear their prayer, Lord. Heal them. Take them as they are and shower upon them Your love, Your forgiveness, Your blessings, Your peace, Your hope, Your renewing power. Although no one today may say they are worthy, when they turn to our God, His grace covers them too. He declares, "You are worthy."

This day we approach the throne of God knowing our true selves, and though many may call us worthy, it is most significant when our Lord, with all of our unworthiness, places upon our lips and our lives His own body and blood, declaring that indeed, by His grace, He declares us worthy.

There is no other Gospel. Jesus, the Christ, the Son of God, the Savior of the world, declares us worthy!

Rev. Vernon D. Gundermann

Independence Day

Rebels and Patriots

Romans 13:1–7

Our text is plain and straightforward. As we consider it, let's also consider a time more than two centuries ago. A new document sat awaiting some of the most prominent men in North America. The craftsmanship of Thomas Jefferson had largely withstood the numerous suggestions and complaints of the Continental Congress. All it needed was John Hancock's "John Hancock" and the signatures of the other delegates. Imagine yourself in line, ready to grasp quill pen and make your mark. What thoughts are in your mind? Do you think of the fighting that started more than a year ago? Do you worry about pledging your life and your possessions plus your "sacred honor" to the cause of independence from England? Are you excited? afraid? uncertain? Hold those thoughts. The line is long, people are moving slowly, and you have time to wait. While waiting, return, if you will, to today's text.

"Let every person be subject to the governing authorities. For there is no authority except from God, and those that exist have been instituted by God" (v. 1). This sounds simple enough. You're a person; I'm a person. Next, governing authorities. Even if you live outside any city limits, you don't live outside the rule of any number of these authorities. Here in these United States, we have mayors and city councils, township officials, county or parish administrators, governors and state legislatures, a president and a Congress. Add to this the judiciary, from city judges to the chief justice of the Supreme Court. We haven't even gotten to the various appointed bureaucrats nor the assorted law-enforcement officers, constables, FBI agents, and all those in-between.

Through Paul, the Holy Spirit reminds us that the offices these men and women hold have been instituted by God. Because God does not govern the world face-to-face—since that would destroy all of us sinful people—He established what we call His "left-hand rule," His "kingdom of the left." He waves His wrathful sword in the face of those who consider criminal activities, often scaring them into compliance (even if they don't agree or wish to cooperate). Others, more bold or more foolish, challenge this rule. They rob, they assault, they threaten and intimidate, they destroy property, sometimes they even kill. For them, God's sword is more than a threat. He authorizes (gives authority to) ordinary people to take extraordinary means. These governing authorities are to forcefully use God's sword. Even the taking of another's life is condoned, so long as it is justly done in the carrying out of this office.

This is what Paul means when he says, "Therefore whoever resists the authorities resists what God has appointed, and those who resist will incur judgment" (v. 2). It's not only the high-profile courtroom dramas where murderers and mass-murderers hear their fate. It's the little everyday things. The eight-sided sign reads "STOP." If you don't stop, don't complain about the police officer writing the ticket. The rectangular sign beside the highway may read 55, 60, or 70. However, if your speedometer reads faster than the sign, don't complain about the police officer writing the ticket.

While you sit beside the road, angry or embarrassed, others blissfully drive past. They aren't worried about being the next person pulled over because they're not speeding. They came to a complete stop. They used their turn signal, didn't block the passing lane, or otherwise kept a law that you broke. They aren't afraid, because "rulers are not a terror to good conduct, but to bad" (v. 3). And in these seemingly minor points, just as much as protecting us from thieves, murderers, or terrorists, each of your divinely instituted governing authorities "is God's servant for your good" (v. 4).

So as you receive your justly deserved ticket for coasting through the stop sign, maybe, either in fear of God or "for the sake of conscience" (v. 5), you imagine if the intersection hadn't been empty. Instead, a van of Little Leaguers, a couple of young girls on bicycles, or an ambulance were there. The authority of your government wanted to make that intersection safe for these and all others.

If we all did as we pleased, the chaos would be unimaginable. Either we would cower in our homes, slipping out only when necessary, or we would be out in oversize vehicles, speeding past, cutting off, or crashing through others. God's servants for your good don't want this to happen any more than you do.

Granted, there are times when government decisions seem ludicrous, even sinful. Strange projects are funded with taxes you've paid. Wars against people who never bothered you drain tax coffers you filled. Laws authorize or allow behavior that we think or know is sinful. In portions of our nation, people can legally indulge in perverse sexual fantasies. They can gamble themselves into debt and poverty. By federal court decisions, they can even end the lives of unborn children in every state of the union.

Yet if the government does not compel us to sin, then "one must be in subjection, not only to avoid God's wrath but also for the sake of conscience" (v. 5). Remember that Paul was looking at a pagan, idolatrous Roman government as his example of authority. Already, some areas faced officially sanctioned persecution of Christians. However, Paul would appeal to this pagan government and its Caesar. He wouldn't attempt a jailbreak, even if unjustly held for more than a year.

Finally, according to Early Church sources, he would bare his neck to the executioner's sword for the crimes of believing in Christ and spreading His Gospel.

Paul wasn't the only one. The martyrs' lists from the Church's first few centuries show person after person who accepted arrest and conviction. They allowed sinful officials to exercise authority even when it meant death. They answered the summons to the stake, the cross, or the arena floor.

Finally, among them all, Old and New Testament martyrs alike, stood the one martyr supreme, to whom they all pointed—Jesus Christ. To this Jesus, the Father gave "all authority" (Mt 28:18). Yet according to His human nature, as a subject of Rome and as an Israelite, Jesus submitted to the authorities. He bore witness of obedience—*martyr* means "witness"—to the Father and to divinely ordered authority.

Christ's perfect obedience, while an example for us, more importantly brings forgiveness for our imperfect, unwilling submission. He was charged the synagogue tax in Capernaum (Mt 17:24–27), which He paid (albeit through the miraculous finding of the coin in the fish). He submitted to the whole Law—moral, ceremonial, and civil—that He Himself handed down on Sinai. He loved God with all His heart, mind, and soul. He loved His neighbor as Himself. He allowed the authorities to arrest Him. He endured the trial of the Jewish council, even if it was held in violation of its own laws. He humbled Himself before Pilate yet also reminded Pilate that even Rome only ruled by divine permission: "You would have no authority over Me at all unless it had been given you from above. Therefore he who delivered Me over to you has the greater sin" (Jn 19:11).

Satan gave Jesus ample opportunity to rebel against the authorities. Imagine him whispering in Jesus' ear, "You're in charge. You have the real authority. Show them who rules!" And that's exactly what Jesus did. He showed all who have eyes to see and ears to hear that His Father ruled. Jesus submitted perfectly to His Father's will, obeying both direct divine command and the will of God exercised through human authority. In so doing, He who was tempted as we are but yet remained "without sin" is able "to sympathize with our weaknesses" (Heb 4:15). He also paid for our weak, sinful disregard of authority.

From all eternity, the Son pledged unending allegiance to the Father. This unswerving loyalty Jesus then displayed also as a man, honoring earthly authority and obeying its laws. This perfect citizen of heaven and earth now confers citizenship rights on us. In Baptism, we have immigrated from the principality of Satan to the kingdom of Christ. As Christ taught His family and His followers, so He teaches us: the Father reigns supreme through His beloved Son.

"All authority in heaven and on earth" belongs to Jesus (Mt 28:18). All creation—believing or not, living or inanimate—is subject to His rule in the kingdom of power. Yet because we are forgiven through the blood of His Son, God blesses us also with citizenship in the kingdom of grace. While the intimidation of divine Law still terrifies us in our sin, the Gospel lovingly draws us closer to our Savior. This forgiveness of sins leads Christians into willing submission to the rule and will of Christ because we know that His rule is perfect and always for our good. He is the King who gave His life for His people. We also willingly are "subject to the governing authorities" (v. 1), because this is right and because we know that it is for our good. We can in good conscience pledge allegiance to our nation's flag and all it represents because we are loyal to the One who rules all nations.

As we circle back to our original consideration, God leads us to an interesting (and, perhaps, uncomfortable) comparison: In a situation almost the reverse of the American Revolution, Jesus came to restore a divine monarchy. He came not only to crush the serpent's head but also to crush the rebellion into which the devil led humankind. His goal was to bring the rebels to surrender or to drive them to flight.

But look, the line has shortened. It's almost your turn. And whether or not to sign this Declaration of Independence is suddenly not as easy a decision as you thought. Are you able to declare in good conscience that the proposed new "governing authorities" have a rule that's "been instituted by God"? Have you perhaps determined that the British government has already forfeited its divine right through neglect and that you're merely ratifying a previous decision? Or, if you sign, might you be violating God's clear message: "Let every person be subject to the governing authorities" (v. 1).

Finally it comes to you. Weighing the Word of God, carefully considering His commands and His promises, you make a decision not only to avoid God's wrath but also for the sake of conscience. What is that decision? No one can tell you. You have been freed by Christ to be a responsible citizen of His earthly and heavenly kingdoms. You know the best decision, and you know that He will empower you to live—even to die—by it. For whatever government you have, no matter how free or oppressed you seem to be, you know that in Christ you are free indeed. Free to live, to love, to serve God, neighbor, and government.

If your choice is made not in spite or in willful disobedience to His Word, then God will either honor it as correct or will forgive a sin done in unwilling ignorance. Christ's obedience both to the governing authorities and to His Father guarantees both.

You don't have to stand there, paralyzed, wondering whether to drop the pen or dip it into the inkwell. Our freedom of choice, coupled with obedience and responsibility to God, goes beyond anything even this great land can offer or guarantee. God's freedom doesn't remove government shackles. Rather, God's freedom allows absolute freedom to be a Christian under earthly government.

For God is a God of order, not chaos, and He continues imposing His rule on all creation. His rule will continue through government as well as Church and Scripture until Christ returns to unite all His "patriots"—we who love our true, eternal Fatherland—into His eternal kingdom of glory, while forever banishing the rebels to the fate they brought on themselves.

God grant you the wisdom to follow just rule and reject the sinful, the ability to pray for those in authority and to thank Him daily for the benefits of stable government, and the desire to use the freedom you now have—as a citizen of the United States and especially as a Christian—to live out your life in honor of Christ and in service of your neighbor. Likewise, the Lord give you courage to use this freedom to proclaim boldly Christ's rule over all and His forgiveness won for all.

Rev. Walter P. Snyder

Independence Day

Pray for All in Authority

1 Timothy 2:1–2

"They are all a bunch of crooks." All of us have heard people say that of our government officials. You yourself have uttered these or similar words. Surveys show that people in our land do not trust their government. On television broadcasts, we have heard people in other lands express the same opinion.

We also know how difficult it is for some children to submit to parental authority. If you are a teen, or if you remember when you were, you must admit that you chafed under parental authority. When a clash of wills occurs, teens feel animosity for their parents.

Because the concept of individual freedom is so strong in our society, many find it difficult to be subject to authority. Even in the workplace some people resent being told what to do. Therefore, it is beneficial on this Fourth of July, when we give thanks for our government, to be reminded to pray for all in authority.

WHO ARE THOSE FOR WHOM WE SHOULD PRAY?

The Scripture for our meditation today urges us to make prayers, intercession, and thanksgiving "for kings and all who are in high positions" (1 Tim 2:2).

If you are a Democrat, you may find it difficult to pray for a Republican president, or vice versa. However, God calls us to pray for the leader of the land, no matter who fills the office. Christians, who believe that God sent His Son to die for all, have a higher reason to pray. Out of love for God, generated by His undeserved love for us, we gladly pray for the spiritual welfare of others, especially that most influential leader, the president.

However, there are many others in authority. There are the members of Congress, federal judges, and other national leaders. We are to intercede also for them. It makes no difference to which political party they belong.

In the state and local governments, the mayor, justices of the peace, and local representatives are among those for whom we pray. The police officer who stops you for a traffic violation is worthy of your respect and prayers. God commands, "Be subject for the Lord's sake to every human institution" (1 Pet 2:13).

Parents have been given authority over their children. "Children, obey your parents in the Lord, for this is right" (Eph 6:1). All of us know that children do not always find it easy to obey, particularly teenagers.

114

Our Savior understands that. He experienced all the stages of life, including the teen years. He became our substitute, obeying God's will in being subject to all authority. The righteousness necessary for eternal life has been earned for us by Christ in all stages of life. God's Word assures us that in Christ we have the righteousness of God (2 Cor 5:21).

In our text, the plural "kings" indicates that we are to pray for the rulers in other countries as well. "There is no authority except from God, and those that exist have been instituted by God" (Rom 13:1), and Jesus said, "Render to Caesar the things that are Caesar's, and to God the things that are God's" (Mk 12:17). God's grace extends toward all people in all places. God so loved the world that He sacrificed His Son, Jesus, for all.

What if the ruler is a tyrant or a dictator? Are we to pray for such an authority also? The two phrases in our text, "all people" and "all," allow for no exceptions; they include everyone who has been placed by God in a position of authority. The criteria for deciding if we should pray for a certain person in authority is not whether we like them or whether we feel they deserve our prayers. In God's sight, outside of Christ there are no good people. All have sinned. All deserve nothing but punishment and eternal damnation. Yet God is good to all—"He makes His sun rise on the evil and on the good, and sends rain on the just and on the unjust" (Mt 5:45).

John the Baptist said of Jesus, "Behold, the Lamb of God, who takes away the sin of the world!" (Jn 1:29). Jesus came to take upon Himself your sins. He has paid the price for your disobedience and rebellion against God. "God shows His love for us in that while we were still sinners, Christ died for us" (Rom 5:8). The Roman Caesar was a tyrant and a pagan. Nevertheless, God said through Paul, "Let every person be subject to the governing authorities. For there is no authority except from God, and those that exist have been instituted by God" (Rom 13:1). The apostle Peter also wrote, "Honor the emperor" (1 Pet 2:17). Therefore, whether good or bad, kind or harsh, rulers need our prayers.

Jesus prayed for those who were treating Him harshly and unfairly. In reality, we were the ones responsible for His suffering and death. As His love and compassion for us penetrates our inmost being, we are led to pray for those who hate and persecute us. Jesus taught, "Love your enemies and pray for those who persecute you" (Mt 5:44). Even if a person in authority becomes our enemy or persecutes us, Christ asks us to pray for that individual.

Why Pray for Those in Authority?

What need do authorities have for our prayers? They are in the driver's seat. Scripture urges us to pray for those in authority so that we can live quiet and peaceful lives. It is the task of government to maintain order so that the Church can carry out our Lord's commission to make disciples of all nations. Without government, which has the authority to punish evildoers, society would be in chaos. Swift and certain punishment helps keep evildoers from committing crimes. For our own sake, therefore, we need to pray that our government officials enact and execute just laws and maintain law and order.

Those who have been entrusted with authority do not always administer fairly. Indeed, one finds many complaints in the Old Testament regarding injustice. "You who afflict the righteous, who take a bribe, and turn aside the needy in the gate" (Amos 5:12). If you have been the victim of injustice administered by some level of government, you know how frustrating that can be. We need to pray for justice in the land for all. God is interested in our temporal as well as our spiritual and eternal welfare.

Sometimes those in authority, be they government, parents, or supervisors in the workplace, act unfairly—by ignorance or by malevolent design. It is not always possible to make the right decisions, especially in difficult cases. It is not possible in every instance to know all the facts. Not all those in authority have the wisdom of Solomon. But we pray for wisdom for those in authority so that they may make decisions that are fair and benefit all of society.

Those in authority often are pressured by rich and powerful people to make decisions favorable to their cause. Most of us are acquainted with such favoritism and conflicts of interest. God complained about the leaders in ancient Israel for giving in to such temptation: "Your princes are rebels and companions of thieves. Everyone loves a bribe and runs after gifts" (Is 1:23). "Power corrupts, and absolute power corrupts absolutely," so the higher the authority, the more our prayers are needed. Pride precedes a fall. Those in authority need our prayers to help them avoid falling for such temptations and injuring society. When we remember that God desires that those in authority be a benefit to us, we are eager to pray that they govern according to His will. As sons and daughters of a merciful God, with His Spirit in us, we desire to help those in authority do their job so that we can do ours—proclaim Jesus Christ, the Savior of the world.

We may not be inclined to pray regularly for those in authority. However, as we remember the blessings that authority brings to our lives, we will find it easier to pray for such people. Look at the many blessings that we have in our country through our form of government. While not perfect, our country has prospered, and the Christian Church has largely been free to go about the task of making disciples of all nations. Imagine what your life would be like without authority. Even those we may dislike and resent the most—whether bosses, parents, or government leaders—are good and necessary. As many children have said in their later years, "At the time I did not appreciate my parents and what they did for me, but now I do."

As we hear and believe that God loves us in Jesus despite our unworthiness, we are moved to respond. God sends the Holy Spirit to empower us to do so. In reverence for God, we submit to His will and walk in His ways. God, in His loving care for us, has provided authorities for our individual good and the good of His Church. May we thank Him joyfully, today and always! Amen.

Rev. Roy H. Bleick

Labor Day

God Establishes Our Work

Psalm 90:17

Labor Day offers occasion for a variety of activities for today's Americans: family get-togethers, house and yard chores, travel.

The U.S. Congress enacted Labor Day as a national holiday in 1894, ordering its observance on the first Monday of September. At that time, working conditions were miserable for the laborer, and management had unrestricted control. A work schedule of twelve hours per day, seven days per week, was common. Benefit packages didn't exist. There was truth to the worker's ballad, "I owe my soul to the company store."[10]

Whatever the conditions, Christians were and are part of the workforce of our land. Although we have protective work laws today, we still run the risk of allowing our work to define our personhood rather than our God-redeemed personhood to define our work. Today's text calls us to recognize that God's gracious favor establishes our work. Because of that, we can (1) give credit where credit is due, (2) learn when to say "when," and (3) be eager to get back to our Lord's work.

GIVE CREDIT WHERE CREDIT IS DUE

Creation's story tells us that God created us for work. "The LORD God took the man and put him in the garden of Eden to work it and keep it" (Gen 2:15). That purposefulness was thwarted by Adam's and Eve's sinful disobedience. Ever since, "cursed is the ground because of you; in pain you shall eat of it all the days of your life; thorns and thistles it shall bring forth for you; and you shall eat the plants of the field. By the sweat of your face you shall eat bread, till you return to the ground, for out of it you were taken; for you are dust, and to dust you shall return" (Gen 3:17–19).

Yet God, in grace, redeems us through the work of His Son, Jesus Christ. In holy love, we are re-created to live as God's people. Moreover, God retools us in the rhythm of work that anticipates rest and rest that anticipates work. He commands, "Six days shall work be done, but the seventh day is a Sabbath of solemn rest, holy to the LORD" (Ex 31:15).

---

10 From the chorus of "Sixteen Tons," © 1947 (Reviewed) Merle's Girls Music (BMI)

Learn When to Say "When"

The contemporary workplace is often plagued by moral and ethical dilemmas, which call for a Christian response. The apostle Paul says in Rom 12:2, "Do not be conformed to this world, but be transformed by the renewal of your mind, that by testing you may discern what is the will of God, what is good and acceptable and perfect." In a society so enthralled with an egalitarian ethic yet so yielding to ever-increasing hierarchical structures, do we remain silent about the loss of personal freedoms to corporate control posing as community consensus? William J. Bennett asks that in a culture that pays "less attention to matters of moral obligation"—personal sacrifice, rules and respect, and propriety and restraint regarding physical pleasure and sexuality—and more to audacious and aggrandizing attitudes accentuating "self-expression, individualism, self-realization, and personal choices," when do we assert that the will of the people is not necessarily the will or work of God?[11] Robert Bork, in *Slouching towards Gomorrah: Modern Liberalism and American Decline*, suggests that, as Christians face "propaganda for every perversion and obscenity imaginable," might not our role as Christ's counterculture be that which delivers our nation from the prospects of "a chaotic and unhappy society, followed, perhaps by an authoritarian and unhappy society"?[12]

Christians bear the cross of Christ in whatever vocation they perform. The bloody sweat of Christ's cross relates to our blood and sweat and tears. The cross provides the motivation for all that we do. "If Jesus' work makes no difference to our work, then we do not belong to Him," says Cary Weisiger.[13]

Work for its own sake, apart from the Lord God, is void of meaning and worth, thus we lament with the writer of Ecclesiastes, "What does man gain by all the toil at which he toils under the sun?" (Eccl 1:3). In this context, Christ abides with His comforting summons, "Come to Me, all who labor and are heavy laden, and I will give you rest" (Mt 11:28). His rest is our eternal "dwelling place, and underneath are the everlasting arms" (Deut 33:27), which sustain us in our endeavors.

Be Eager to Get Back to Our Lord's Work

There is purpose to our work. Christians participate in God's working and experience—what Paul Bretscher calls "the delight of having ideas and turning them

---

11 William J. Bennett, "What to Do about . . . The Children," in *What to Do About . . .*, ed. by Neal Kozodoy (New York: Regan Books, 1995), 5.

12 Robert H. Bork, *Slouching towards Gomorrah: Modern Liberalism and American Decline* (New York: Harpercollins, 1996), 139.

13 Cary N. Weisiger III, *The Epistles of Peter* (Grand Rapids: Baker, 1961), 52.

into reality."[14] Not to work is to deprive ourselves or others of God's benefits. Each believer must "labor, doing honest work with his own hands, so that he may have something to share with anyone in need" (Eph 4:28).

Work connects us to Jesus' harvesting of blood-bought souls. He uses us in His fields, which "are white for harvest" (Jn 4:35). Whatever our field might be, each of us "goes out to his work and to his labor until the evening" (Ps 104:23). Jesus sends us "to reap that for which you did not labor" always reminding us that "others have labored, and you have entered into their labor" (Jn 4:38). Although we are transient, God makes our efforts effective and enduring. He makes us a part of the harvest; He continues to use us to reap. Therefore, we are "always abounding in the work of the Lord, knowing that in the Lord [our] labor is not in vain" (1 Cor 15:58).

Christians work eagerly because it demonstrates dependence on God's direction of its every detail. "For by grace you have been saved through faith. And this is not your own doing; it is the gift of God, not a result of works, so that no one may boast. For we are His workmanship, created in Christ Jesus for good works, which God prepared beforehand, that we should walk in them" (Eph 2:8–10). Diversity of duty underscores our unity in Christ. "Whatever you do, in word or deed, do everything in the name of the Lord Jesus, giving thanks to God the Father through Him" (Col 3:17) and "work heartily, as for the Lord and not for men" (Col 3:23).

Every day for us is a Labor Day in Christ, who has the master plan designed for us. In accord with His plan for our salvation, we stay in touch for daily adjustments. Dietrich Bonhoeffer helps us remember that each day we both pray and work, because these functions define our days. Bonhoeffer also points out that through our prayers, God strengthens us to faithfully go about our daily tasks.[15]

One day at a time we pray: "Thus, Lord Jesus, ev'ry task Be to You commended; May Your will be done, I ask, Until life is ended. Jesus, in Your name begun Be the day's endeavor; Grant that it may well be done To Your praise forever" (LSB 869:5).[16]

Rev. William L. Couch

---

14 Paul G. Bretscher, *The Foolishness of God* (Valparaiso, IN: Immanuel Curriculum, 1987), 31.

15 Dietrich Bonhoeffer, *Life Together* (New York: Harper & Row, 1954), 69–71.

16 Text copyright © 1941 Concordia Publishing House. All rights reserved.

Labor Day

Whistle While You Work

Colossians 3:14–17

Tomorrow, by the grace of God, we will once again observe Labor Day throughout the United States, Puerto Rico, and Canada. It's a day to honor working men and women all over our country. Labor organizations sponsor various celebrations and parades. Yet for most people it is a day of rest and recreation. It has also become a symbol of the end of summer. Two men have been credited with suggesting a holiday to honor working people in the United States: Matthew Maguire, a machinist from New Jersey, and Peter J. McGuire, a New York City carpenter. Both men played an important part in staging the first Labor Day parade in New York City in September 1882. President Grover Cleveland signed a bill in 1894 making Labor Day a national holiday.

While Labor Day is a celebration to honor working people, we Christians need to ask ourselves, How do we see work? Do we see ourselves as hired help, so that our day-to-day work is nothing more than a necessary evil so that we can really enjoy life during our time off? So often, rather than seeing every aspect of our lives as an exciting opportunity to honor God, we see work and our jobs as drudgery.

Contrary to this type of attitude, God's Holy Word sees things from a different perspective and in a different light. As we comb the pages of the Scriptures, we find many examples of how our Lord wants us to conform our attitudes toward work to His concept of work. True, God wants us to rest. He wants us to relax and enjoy life, but that doesn't mean that we see work as drudgery. No, quite the contrary, God wants us to find contentment in everything we do, to approach every aspect of our day-to-day tasks with a good heart—whether our work is the study of a student; the house work essential to the well-being of every family; a job in a factory; an office position; sales on the road; or even the task of finding work. Paul says, "Whatever you do, in word or deed, do everything in the name of the Lord Jesus" (v. 17).

Work is good for us. In the beginning, God created a perfect world. Everything was beautiful and wonderful. In Genesis 1, ten times we read the phrase, "God said . . . and it was so." That phrase is more than a mere introduction with poetic license. It is the truth of our God, who put everything in perfect order: the heavens and the earth, the moon and the stars, the seas and everything in them, the land, the plants, and the animals. The crown of God's creation was man. God, with His own almighty hand, created man from the dust of the earth and fashioned Him in His own perfect image. "Male and female He created them," Gen 1:27 tells us.

But God did not create man and woman simply to sit around and watch everything happen. In the later part of Genesis 1, God gives Adam and Eve directions for work. They are to be fruitful and multiply; rule over the land, the birds, the fish, and every living creature on the earth; and care for all creation. "The LORD God took the man and put him in the garden of Eden to work it and keep it" (Gen 2:15). So work is not a mere invention of man, but is ordained by God, and God blesses the various labors of people everywhere.

Through sin, though, work has become difficult. Adam and Eve succumbed to the temptations of the evil one. Doubting God's Word and promise, they desired to be like God. They acted against the Word and command of God. After their sinful act, God said to Eve, "I will surely multiply your pain in childbearing; in pain you shall bring forth children" (Gen 3:16). He said to Adam, "Cursed is the ground because of you; in pain you shall eat of it all the days of your life; thorns and thistles it shall bring forth for you; and you shall eat the plants of the field. By the sweat of your face you shall eat bread, till you return to the ground, for out of it you were taken; for you are dust, and to dust you shall return" (Gen 3:17–19). Work, before the fall, was a joyful experience that was blessed by God. Work, after the fall, is tiring and hard because of sin, but it is still good and beneficial.

The problem—with us and with our work—is sin. Our sin separates us from God, and from the abundant life that God prepared for us. In fact, our very attitudes, twisted away from God and from love of our neighbor, become part of the problem. When we look at our work only as burdensome menial tasks, our attitude is not what God wants it to be. We sin not only by our actions but also in our thoughts and our words.

But Scripture tells us, "For as by the one man's disobedience the many were made sinners, so by the one man's obedience the many will be made righteous" (Rom 5:19). The contrast here is clear. Adam introduced sin and death into the world, but Jesus Christ brings righteousness and life. Adam brought condemnation, but Jesus Christ brings justification. Adam died and returned to the dust, but after Jesus died, taking all of our sins upon Himself, He rose in glory. The Holy Spirit gives us faith to believe in Jesus and His salvation. The result is that we desire to serve our Lord in everything we do and say and think! The work of the Holy Spirit changes our actions and attitudes.

We then see work as a blessing of God. It is an opportunity for us to serve God and our neighbor. Work is not merely a necessary evil, something to do so we can have a home, a car, food, and clothing—though our work normally does provide those things. But, as Paul wrote to Timothy, "there is great gain in godliness with contentment, for we brought nothing into the world, and we cannot take anything out of the world. But if we have food and clothing, with these we will be content. But those who desire to be rich fall into temptation, into a snare, into many senseless and harmful desires that plunge people into ruin and destruction" (1 Tim 6:6–9). We need, indeed, to thank God daily for His blessings and see the many opportunities He lays before us. We need to give thanks to God for the opportunity to work.

Work is an opportunity for us to witness. The Disney fantasy classic *Snow White and the Seven Dwarfs* shows a picture of a positive attitude toward work. Remember the dwarfs, who would whistle and sing while they were at work? Now I'm certainly not advocating that Doc, Sleepy, Dopey, Grumpy, or the others are giving us a biblical directive here, but if Disney can promote a positive attitude toward work, how much more can we Christians? We know that work is good for us, that it is a blessing given by God for our own health of mind and body and to supply our needs. With that attitude we see work as an opportunity to serve and to witness.

The Colossian Church was a predominately Gentile congregation in the midst of pagans. There was religious activity all around them, as people were enamored with false gods and spiritual philosophies. Even in the midst of their own congregation, there was a heresy that attacked the total adequacy and unique supremacy of Jesus Christ. In response to this, Paul emphasizes the doctrine of creation and how all things were created through Christ, in whom the fullness of the Godhead dwells. He shows how Jesus Christ, the great God-man, needs to be the central focus of their lives.

Our God cares about us and what we do. He is personally involved in each of us and lovingly cares for all of us. He puts us on the top of His priority list, and He wants to be on the top of ours. Paul says, "Let the peace of Christ rule in your hearts. . . . Whatever you do, in word or deed, do everything in the name of the Lord Jesus" (vv. 15, 17). Here he uses a Greek verb that originally meant "to award a prize in an athletic contest" and then came to mean "be umpire or judge; decide, control, rule": "Let the peace of God umpire your hearts." Christianity is a day-to-day thing, not just a "church thing" that you do once each week as you suffer through one bitter hour. Our Christian faith is to be applied to every aspect of our daily living.

Today many of you will relax while watching the great American pastime: baseball. Maybe some of you will even play baseball or softball. Behind the plate or in the field will stand the umpire. He calls balls and strikes. He tells the players if they are safe or out. His decision is final, no matter how much you argue with him.

123

The peace that comes from our God through the Gospel of Jesus Christ, tells us that we are safe in the loving arms of the great Shepherd of the sheep, who truly cares for us. He gives us His Holy Spirit so that His peace is the umpire in everything we do and say, whether at home, at church, with family and friends, and yes, even at work. Our work is an opportunity for us to serve our God and to share His love. God directs us so that we are not high and outside, low in the dirt, a wild pitch, or a mean-spirited "bean ball." Our God directs us with His peace and love so that we are right down the middle!

Faithful stewards are those "rendering service with a good will as to the Lord and not to man" (Eph 6:7). However lowly or unrecognized a job may be, it can be done for the Lord. It is reported that Martin Luther said, "The housemaid on her knees scrubbing the floor is doing a work as pleasing in the eye of almighty God as the priest on his knees before the altar saying Mass."

We serve our Lord in every aspect of our lives as a loving response to the Gospel of peace that He has so lavishly and graciously bestowed upon us. We need to ask ourselves, "Does my attitude please my God? How would I work and act differently if Jesus were standing next to me? Can I say this in the same breath as the name of Jesus Christ?" With joy in our heart and soul, we do everything in our life to the glory of our Lord.

Hum a spiritual song as you go to work each day. Whistle while you work. Sing a joyful tune on your way home. Paul tells us to be "singing psalms and hymns and spiritual songs, with thankfulness in your hearts to God" (v. 16). Let this attitude dwell in you richly, as the Holy Spirit gives you ability. "And whatever you do, in word or deed, do everything in the name of the Lord Jesus, giving thanks to God the Father through Him" (v. 17). Joyfully do your work to the glory of God, giving thanks for the ability to labor. Then the words "Happy Labor Day" will be more than a wish—they will be a joyful reality in the Lord.

Rev. James K. Gullen

Veterans Day

God's Grace Is Never Cheap

2 Samuel 1:19, 24–25a; Romans 5:8

GRACE IS A COSTLY GIFT

Inscribed near the entrance of a cemetery in Okinawa, where many U.S. military personnel are buried, are these words: "We gave our todays in order that you might have your tomorrows." Veterans Day is a time to remember that much of what we enjoy in life comes to us through the service and sacrifice of others. In fact, God's grace often comes to us through others. And, most certainly, God's grace is never cheap!

There is a moving song written by David in the Old Testament that especially emphasizes that truth. God had chosen David as Israel's future king, and he was immensely popular among the people after he had killed the giant Goliath. Unfortunately, the reigning King Saul became obsessed with jealousy over David and repeatedly tried to kill him. David tried to assure Saul of his allegiance. Even David's dear friend Jonathan, Saul's son, tried desperately to restore this broken relationship. But it was all to no avail. David was forced to live as a fugitive, constantly on the run and in fear for his life.

Then, in 2 Samuel 1, a tattered and exhausted messenger arrived at the camp where David was hiding with a band of his followers. The messenger brought the news that both Saul and Jonathan had been killed in battle. As proof, he handed David a band from the king's arm and, the most prized possession, the king's crown.

One could naturally assume that David, after he had heard this news and received the crown, was overwhelmed with joy. After all, he was now free from danger. And, more important, the wicked and deranged king was dead, and the path to the throne was finally cleared. Instead, David mourned bitterly over the news and composed a heart-wrenching song that reflected his grief. Throughout the song, a powerful phrase recurs: "How the mighty have fallen. . . . How the mighty have fallen!"

Those are not words of gloating, but words of deep lament. David recognized that much of what his nation enjoyed came through the service and sacrifice of Saul. "You daughters of Israel, weep over Saul, who clothed you luxuriously in scarlet, who put ornaments of gold on your apparel. How the mighty have fallen in the midst of the battle!" (2 Sam 1:24–25).

GRACE IS A DAILY GIFT

None of us fully grasps the total cost of God's grace in our lives. Sometimes we speak almost casually about the sacrifice of Jesus Christ for our salvation. But if we don't even notice the day-to-day sacrifices in our behalf, how can we begin to appreciate the incomprehensible incarnation and vicarious suffering of the Son of God for us? Remember, God's grace is never cheap!

Recall, for example, the simple graces or undeserved blessings we've already enjoyed this day. That warm cup of coffee and the banana on our cereal—how many faceless and dirt-poor people made that possible? Or the clothing on our backs—how much of it came from sweatshops in third-world countries? Then there are the untold hundreds who make possible the gas and oil that fuel our cars and the discreet disappearance of our garbage and sewage. When you begin to review everything in your life, the list of struggling contributors becomes over-whelming. "Who clothed you luxuriously in scarlet, who put ornaments of gold on your apparel"? God's grace is never cheap!

And who, fellow Americans, has made it possible for us to travel wherever we please, to speak whatever we think, to read whatever we want, to worship anyway we please, and to elect whomever we choose? Has any of that come to us without cost? Do we ever consider the scores, hundreds, thousands of lives that have, in some way, been sacrificed for our moments of comfort this day, which we take so much for granted?

Some time ago, when the motion picture *Saving Private Ryan* came out, there was a brief renewal of interest in the experiences of our veterans. Many were motivated by the movie to delve into the details of the 1944 D-Day Normandy landing. They discovered that by sundown on that day, forty thousand Americans had stormed the beaches, and one in every nineteen persons had become a casualty. The Normandy invasion was one of unimaginable slaughter, worse than most of us ever realized.

Saving Private Ryan was the story of a squad of rangers sent to save a man whose three brothers had been killed in battle. Decision-makers wanted him sent home to spare his mother the agony of losing all of her sons. They find Ryan but are caught in a fierce battle, and the squad's leader is mortally wounded. With his final breath, he whispers to Ryan, "Earn this." Obviously, no matter how "good" Ryan would live for all the years to come, he could never earn that for which those men had sacrificed their lives.

GRACE IS ALWAYS AN UNDESERVED GIFT

"Earn this!" We can't, of course. We can never earn the grace under which we all live. But God forbid that we should ever ignore the cost! "What do you have that you did not receive?" asked Paul of the Corinthians. "If then you received it," he adds, "why do you boast as if you did not receive it?" (1 Cor 4:7). Veterans Day is a time for remembering the priceless grace of God in so many small things and, through that, to begin to grasp more fully what His grace through the sacrifice of Christ in our behalf really means.

What happened at Normandy, regrettably, has been repeated again and again—at the Chosin Reservoir, Da Nang, the Gulf War. Even when our nation is not at war, U.S. servicemen and servicewomen are often killed or wounded while aiding our allies or protecting our borders. Are all those who die or are wounded in such service righteous? No. In fact, not one of them is. They are no more righteous than those who slaved to provide our coffee, bananas, clothing, fuel, or sanitation. They are no more righteous than we are. But each was or is a precious child of God. "How the mighty have fallen!" And we have benefited because of their suffering through no merit on our part whatsoever. God's grace is never cheap!

GRACE IS THE ULTIMATE DIVINE GIFT

When we live in that kind of awareness—the kind of awareness that David had at the news of Saul's death—we begin to get a faint glimpse of what Paul was talking about in Romans 5. "But God shows His love for us in that while we were still sinners, Christ died for us" (v. 8). In fact, as Paul put it, God intervened in history "at the right time," namely, "while we were still weak" (v. 6).

In one sense, we are all fugitives like David—constantly on the run, always living under the threat of death. Try as we may, we can never appease a righteous and jealous God who seeks total allegiance. Even as we attempt to do good works we know, truthfully, how short we fall of the demand, "Be perfect, as your heavenly Father is perfect" (Mt 5:48).

Then, inconceivably, we receive the most unexpected news. The King has been killed in our stead, and we are now offered the crown of life! God's grace is new to us every morning—showering us with so many undeserved blessings. But nothing can compare to this, namely, that the very King of heaven, our Lord Jesus Christ, died in our place, and we have been elevated like kings, inheriting a kingdom He prepared for us from the beginning of time. Moreover, the One who sacrificed Himself for us was and is, for the most part, rejected, which adds to the wonder of this gift.

Among the veterans we honor this day are the Japanese Americans who fought so valiantly for our country during World War II. They were referred to as "Nisei" in those days and originally classified by the draft board as 4-C, a code for "enemy alien." Yet many of those young men insisted on serving in order to demonstrate their love for their country. Many died, thousands were wounded, but despite their heroism and sacrifice, many were never granted the honor they deserved at the end of the war. It took nearly a half-century for our country to overcome its unfounded rejection of these fellow citizens and, finally, in the year 2000, to grant the Medal of Honor to twenty-one of them for their well-documented and unprecedented bravery. Sadly, by the time the award was given, only nine of them were still living.

The prophet Isaiah said of our Lord: "He was despised and rejected by men; a man of sorrows, and acquainted with grief; and as one from whom men hide their faces He was despised, and we esteemed Him not. Surely He has borne our griefs and carried our sorrows; yet we esteemed Him stricken, smitten by God, and afflicted. But He was wounded for our transgressions; He was crushed for our iniquities; upon Him was the chastisement that brought us peace, and with His stripes we are healed" (Is 53:3–5). At what tremendous cost God has given us His grace!

Grace Is a Life-Changing Gift

When you become conscious of the grace of God in your life through daily blessings, and then begin to see the far more wondrous thing of God's grace in Jesus Christ, your whole demeanor and approach to life begin to change. That was the case for John Newton, the captain of a slave ship in the late 1700s. He had led a despicable life, participating in virtually every evil one could imagine. But he was spared from a malignant fever in Africa and a terrifying storm at sea. Those experiences, coupled with his reading of Thomas à Kempis's *The Imitation of Christ*, opened his eyes. He ultimately became a great hymn writer, and his best-known work sums up his life:

> Amazing grace—how sweet the sound—
> That saved a wretch like me!
> I once was lost, but now am found,
> Was blind but now I see! (*LSB* 744:1)

Like David's song "How the mighty have fallen," the hymn "Amazing Grace" is no gloating boast of a victor. It is a tear-filled memory of the One who died in our place so that we might live forever. How can we ever repay such, other than with choking sobs: "How the mighty have fallen." It changes one's life. "Beloved, if God so loved us, we also ought to love one another" (1 Jn 4:11).

Veterans Day is a time to honor all our veterans for all they have secured for us. But it is also a day of vivid reminders of God's total grace in our lives—not only in the daily treasures we have but also, and especially, in the crown of life, which is ours through Jesus Christ. We can call it "amazing," "wondrous," "boundless"—but there really is no adjective to describe its cost. Above all, it is not now, nor has it ever been, cheap! The amount paid for who we are now and what we shall be in eternity is beyond comprehension. Certainly, that realization transforms our lives, and we are moved to praise Him in all that we do and say.

Is it any wonder that in St. John's vision of heaven the "numbering myriads of myriads and thousands of thousands" of angels encircling Christ were thunderously singing, "Worthy is the Lamb who was slain, to receive power and wealth and wisdom and might and honor and glory and blessing!" (Rev 5:11–12). And eventually, says John, every creature on earth and in heaven will join in singing: "To Him who sits on the throne and to the Lamb be blessing and honor and glory and might forever and ever!" (v. 13).

Rev. Rodger R. Venzke

Veterans Day

Serving Breakfast

Jeremiah 29:7

The chatter in the barnyard one morning got around to the farmer's current bout with the flu bug. "It's a shame he's so sick," mooed the cow. "Now Mrs. Farmer has to do his chores as well as hers."

"Yes," neighed the horses, "she needs someone to help her."

"Of course she does," the chicken cackled, "and it ought to be us. We're the ones the chores help. We ought to get involved!"

All the animals noised their agreement: "Yes! Sure! Right on! We're with you."

"But what can we do?" the collie questioned.

They all scratched for an idea. "I've got it!" cheered the chicken. "Tomorrow morning let's make breakfast for them. We'll fix bacon and eggs! I'll lay the eggs."

"Well, forget about me, then," snorted the pig, "I don't want to get that involved!"

Today we honor involvement that sometimes does cost the lives of those involved. We join with all the United States in saluting the men and women—regular and reserve; active, discharged, and retired; alive or departed—who have served in our armed forces: the Army, the Navy, the Air Force, the Marines, and the Coast Guard. These people truly have been involved! They did their chores for the rest of us, and we enjoy more peace and prosperity because of them. For that we thank them, and we thank God!

Some of them were involved in providing the eggs; they survived. Others provided the bacon; they died doing it.

On an occasion like this we are vividly aware of the difference. To those of you who provided some of those eggs in the military and to those of you whose loved ones did so, we say to you personally and sincerely, "Thank you." To those of you whose loved ones died in military service, we want to say more than "Thank you." We grope to understand what it means to provide the bacon. We want to shed a tear as we try.

It is fitting to look back and applaud these heroes on Veterans Day. Our celebration cannot, however, end there. After all, the whole point of the bacon and eggs was to provide breakfast for someone else. We need to look around to see if we are "eating the breakfast of freedom" that our armed forces have served up at such great expense. Are you? Are others around you in this congregation? in this community? in this city?

God punished the Israelites for their idolatry against Him by sending them into exile in Babylon. He took away their freedom. Then He told Jeremiah to write a letter. You'll find it in chapter 29, and our text is taken from it. God told His people that no one was going to come home for seventy years, so they should settle down and work for the well-being of the cities where they were. Why? Because, as the welfare of the city goes, so goes their welfare.

That is also true of us. The welfare of our church is profoundly affected by the condition of our city and country, and vice versa, so we are to pray for our communities and actively seek their good. As with the Israelites under the Babylonian government, church and state are separate today, but they are dramatically influenced by each other. We must become involved to ensure that that influence is good.

When Benjamin Franklin returned to his shop after the Continental Congress, one of his clients asked him, "Well, Mr. Franklin, I see you're back. And what have you brought us?" To which the statesman replied, "A republic, madam, if you can keep it."

Keeping the welfare of our nation under God remains one of our tasks in (year) as well. It is the "breakfast" that the founding fathers and more than two hundred years of veterans have provided for us.

Are you eating that breakfast? How are you exercising your U.S. citizenship? Are you a registered voter? Do you show up to vote? Are you recycling? Are you giving time to any charity? Are you part of a neighborhood watch or some other anti-crime program? Do you support block homes in the area? Are you active in your child's school? Do you attend meetings of your local governing body? Do you tell your elected officials what you think is good for your city? Do you keep informed about how your city, state, and country are dealing with the major issues of the day? Have you ever considered running for public office? If you do nothing—and other good citizens do nothing—then what will happen to the welfare of your community? What will become of the bacon and eggs that others have served us?

God is a veteran at getting involved and fixing breakfast too. He has personally taken part in the battle caused by human sin. The apostle James reminds us of this battle. After pointing out the difference between disruptive, so-called "wisdom" and peacemaking wisdom, he asks, "What causes quarrels and what causes fights among you? Is it not this, that your passions are at war within you?" (James 4:1).

So it has been, and so it still is. From Adam and Eve, through Joseph, Rahab, the Samaritan woman at the well, the Pharisee praying in the temple, the plundering of the Huns, the marauding armies of the Hundred Years' War, the conquests of colonialism, the oppressive side of the industrial revolution, world wars to "end all war," down to our own urban violence and the war on terrorism, the wounds of war scar our histories.

Nor are all wars fought in other times and in other places. Many of them are under our nose: shopping mall muggings, spouse and child abuse, arguments over morality in neighborhoods, tensions over a parish decision, smoldering animosities in an office, territorialism in a factory, chilling standoffs in a home. Any of these mini-wars can paralyze and scar us.

And as if it is not enough that we war against one another, humankind has warred against God since Eden. We Christians today know that our sinful nature opposes what God intends for us. We always need relief from such war. St. Paul moans for all of us, "I delight in the law of God, in my inner being, but I see in my members another law waging war against the law of my mind and making me captive to the law of sin that dwells in my members. Wretched man that I am! Who will deliver me from this body of death? Thanks be to God through Jesus Christ our Lord!" (Rom 7:22–25).

So what did God, against whom we have transgressed, do? He fixed breakfast for us! He sent His only Son to be our bacon and eggs. Look again at His recipe:

> He came at Christmas and took on our human form. How we celebrate that with excitement and bells!

> He lived among us, caring, healing, forgiving, teaching, and finally feeding us with His body and blood, given and shed for our salvation. How deeply we sense His presence among us when we receive Him in the Sacrament (as we will do today).

> He died in our place—God's ultimate involvement! He died to do for us what we could never do for ourselves. He prepared that breakfast feast we will share with Him in heaven.

> He rose again on Easter, and so shall we rise when He returns! This is God's house specialty, heaven's grand slam, eternity's fireworks! Our Lord's resurrection—and His assurance of ours—sparks every Sunday worship. It comforts us at every Christian graveside. It echoes Christ's words to His disciples on Maundy Thursday evening, "In My Father's house are many rooms. If it were not so, would I have told you that I go to prepare a place for you? And if I go and prepare a place for you, I will come again and will take you to Myself, that where I am you may be also" (Jn 14:2–3).

This is the Gospel! This is Christianity's core! This is God's own involvement, His bacon and eggs, heaven's own breakfast for you!

As Veterans Day is fully honored both by recalling the past sacrifices and service and by rolling up our sleeves to preserve the welfare of our nation, so also our Lord's salvation is fully honored both by praising Him for all He has done, as we are doing this morning, and by rolling up our sleeves to share God's forgiving grace with others, as we will have several chances to do so this week.

In that spirit, let's think about ways we can become involved this week. For whom can we fix breakfast? Some may be reluctant to risk self-sacrifice, to supply the bacon, but our Lord, who sacrificed His very life, calls us to lose our life for His sake in order to find it. Ask yourselves,

Whom do I know who is sick and in need of a visit and a few minutes of my company?

Whom do I know who is grieving over a wayward youth and in need of my understanding and encouragement?

Whom do I know who is cringing inside because his or her parents don't understand the confusions tugging at a teenager's life—someone who desperately needs a few hugs of understanding?

Whom do I know who is wandering aimlessly in spirit because his or her career is hollow or unproductive?

Whom do I know who is so ashamed of something he or she has said or done that God's forgiveness seems out of reach?

Whom do I know who is looking for God's love and peace in his or her life?

Whom do I know who needs to be invited to come along next Sunday to be blessed by the worship and fellowship of this congregation?

You know better than I do the answers to these questions. You, dear friends, have your own homework for this week.

On the one hand, you have the welfare of your own city to seek and, in turn, a little bit of the welfare of this country. On the other hand, you also have the welfare of God's kingdom to seek and spiritually hungry souls to look for. Christ has already supplied the bacon by giving His life; you and I are to supply the eggs by sharing the faith that God's Spirit has put within us. To whom will you serve our Lord's bacon and eggs this week?

Dr. Richard D. Labore

Veterans Day

The Perfect Shield

Ephesians 6:10–17

War is usually not one of our favorite topics of discussion. Although God can and does use war to protect nations, to free captive people, and to restrict evil, war also brings suffering. It produces heartache and destruction. The Civil War General William Tecumseh Sherman put it in the strongest terms: "War is at best barbarism. Its glory is all moonshine. It is only those who have neither fired a shot nor heard the shrieks and groans of the wounded who cry aloud for blood, more vengeance, more desolation. War is hell."

Most of us don't think about war often. One reason is that historically North Americans have been isolationists. We've focused more on what we need to do here to take care of our families and communities and nation and less on what we might need to do over there to deal with a possible enemy. That's good. A second reason North Americans usually don't think about war is that war is painful. War bothers reasonable people so much that they would prefer not to think about it. In fact, as North Americans, if we're not at war, we tend to think wishfully that our enemy isn't even real.

That's one of the reasons that the events of September 11, 2001, stunned so many of us. Essentially, we didn't believe that the terrorist enemy was real. As a nation, we may have witnessed the August 1998 bombings of the U.S. embassies in Nairobi, Kenya, and Dar es Salaam, Tanzania. Hundreds were murdered, but somehow it was a "problem in Africa." And as a nation, we may have witnessed the October 2000 bombing of the USS *Cole* in Yemen. Seventeen sailors were killed, but somehow it was an "isolated, tragic event."

Then, finally, when three thousand people were killed in the 9/11 terrorist attacks in the United States, the evidence was undeniable. There were thousands of bodies at the World Trade Center, the Pentagon, and on United Airlines Flight 93, which crashed in Somerset County, Pennsylvania. We could no longer wish away the enemy. The enemy was real! There were terrorists who were actively recruiting, training, planning, and carrying out a war against the United States. In their evil, these terrorists continue to search out ways to kill as many U.S. residents—men, women, and children—as possible. This is why the United States went to war against Iraq and continues to pursue the global war on terror. This, too, is why we need a shield against our enemies. In fact, considering which very real enemies we face, we need the perfect shield.

Because the United States, and the freedom for which it stands, always has had enemies, we, as a nation, set aside a day to honor the veterans of our armed forces. In Romans 13, St. Paul declares that God ordains governments, which in turn establish the military. Soldiers, sailors, pilots, marines, and coastguard personnel are servants of God. They are God's servants, not in the sense of preaching the Gospel to save souls for heaven, but in the sense of using military force to establish order and justice on earth. They do God's work by punishing those who do wrong, by protecting those who need protecting, and ultimately by paving the way for a just and lasting peace.

Military service is not easy. It requires much: long, hard hours of training; deployments in the cold, the hot, the rain, the snow, the mud, the sand; lack of sleep and creature comforts; separation from family. To this, veterans add the courage, the integrity, and the selfless service to do all that is needed, even to lay down one's life, if necessary. Family members are a part of the team, for God also calls them to serve—to provide an anchor for the family and community and to bear up their service members in support and prayer. If you have served in the armed forces or been a family member who supported a service person, I thank you on behalf of a grateful nation. It wasn't always easy, but you paid the price for freedom. If you are young, I would encourage you to consider taking up this noble and God-pleasing service. The enemy is real, and we need such selfless servants.

It is true: we'd prefer to think we don't have an enemy. War brings so much pain, death, and destruction. War means that an enemy has us in his sights. Unless we see missiles flying or hear incoming artillery, we're tempted to think wishfully that the enemy isn't real. But he is.

Spiritually, it's the same. Think about your spiritual enemy. Satan and his evil devils are more powerful than you are. They are more cunning than you are. They have one objective: to kill you eternally in hell. That thought can be so terrifying that we're tempted to think wishfully that our enemy isn't real! After all, when was the last time you saw Satan attack, wound, and kill someone? It can just sound like too much "spiritualizing."

Sadly, the evidence shows that our enemy is real. Despite knowing that you should fear, love, and trust in God above all things, what do you do? Do you forget about God, trusting more in yourself and in your own wits each day? Do you curse, swear, or otherwise misuse the name of the Lord? Do you ignore His Word as the source of life and Spirit? If you're a son or daughter, do you despise God's gift of parents, disrespecting and dishonoring them? If you're married, do you mock God's good gift of marriage by bad-mouthing your spouse if not by being unfaithful? The list could go on and on.

With such great gifts from God, what could account for your disrespect, dishonor, and destruction of such blessings? The evidence points to the fact that the enemy is real. The enemy is influencing you powerfully on the spiritual battlefield. "For we do not wrestle against flesh and blood, but against the rulers, against the authorities, against the cosmic powers over this present darkness, against the spiritual forces of evil in the heavenly places" (Eph 6:12).

Which is why we need a shield to protect us.

From the beginning of warfare, man has devised shields to protect him in battle. Shields were made of wood, then leather, and then metal as technology progressed. The most advanced military shield in the U.S. arsenal is the Patriot missile; it continues to be improved with what is called "PAC 3" technology.

One of our Lutheran Church—Missouri Synod army chaplains probably wouldn't be alive today except for the grace of God and the shield of a Patriot missile during the 1991 Gulf War. As a SCUD missile was coming down onto his position at King Abdul Aziz Airport, two Patriot missiles were launched. The first one passed the incoming SCUD, did a U-turn, came back, and exploded it overhead in the sky. A few fragments fell, but he and his fellow soldiers were shielded.

Yet as good a shield as the Patriot is, it isn't perfect. Toward the end of the Gulf War, one SCUD got through and hit a barracks outside Dharan, killing twenty-eight soldiers and wounding ninety-eight more. The Patriot was good, but it was not the perfect shield. Not only in war but also in daily life we need shields. Education is a gift of God. It protects us from ignorance and poverty. Yet some of the most educated people know nothing of God and His love. Education is not the perfect shield.

Family and friends are wonderful gifts from God. They protect us from loneliness and isolation. Yet so many people who have been given so much consume family and friends like a drunk might consume a bottle of alcohol and throw it away. Family and friends generally protect us well, but they are not the perfect shield.

Especially because Satan and his evil angels have targeted you and me, we need the perfect shield. That perfect shield is God.

God first announced that He was the perfect shield to Abram. God told him, "I am your shield" (Gen 15:1). Abram, later named Abraham, had real worries and real enemies. Foreign armies had planned to conquer him. Foreign kings had threatened to kill him. And though God Himself had given Him the messianic promise, that through Abram would come a Son who would bless the entire world, Abram was 75 years old and still childless. It was precisely at this time that God told Abram, "Fear not, Abram, I am your shield."

Indeed, the Son of Abraham, the Son of God, has come. His name is Jesus. By God's grace through faith, He is our perfect shield. As St. Paul says, "In all circumstances take up the shield of faith, with which you can extinguish all the flaming darts of the evil one" (Eph 6:16). What are these "flaming arrows" that Christ, our perfect shield, can stop for us?

The name of the first flaming arrow is uncertainty. Since the beginning, Satan has attacked with the arrow of uncertainty. In the Garden of Eden, after God had created everything for man to enjoy but put one tree, the tree of the knowledge of good and evil, off-limits, Satan's first question to Eve was, "Has God told you that you shouldn't eat of any of the trees?" His attack was designed to make Eve uncertain of God and what He had said.

So, too, in our life Satan tempts us with uncertainty. Satan asks: God's Ten Commandments have some wiggle room, don't they? Do you really have to fear, love, and trust in God above all things? Won't God understand if you occasionally take His name in vain? Can't you set God's Word aside for a little while and not worry about hearing it, believing it, or living it? Do you have to honor and obey all authorities? Can't you just let your needy neighbor fend for himself? Do you really have to honor your spouse for life? Don't you have a right to "pinch" a little bit here or there, so long as what you take won't hurt others too much? Is gossiping against your neighbor really that bad? Do you have to be satisfied with whatever God gives you?

Satan's arrow of uncertainty is aimed at you so that you will be uncertain of God and what He commands. Maybe God has only given you Ten Suggestions, and you really don't have to obey them. You can bend them according to your will.

Christ, our perfect shield, stops this flaming arrow. In His Sermon on the Mount, He makes God's Law crystal clear: "Truly, I say to you, until heaven and earth pass away, not an iota, not a dot, will pass from the Law until all is accomplished. . . . Unless your righteousness exceeds that of the scribes and Pharisees, you will never enter the kingdom of heaven" (Mt 5:18, 20). The Ten Commandments stand as God's absolute Law. Christ says this is true, period, and that you must obey God's Law.

The truth of God's Law is foundational. Knowing what God absolutely commands helps you fight the enemy and not be fooled by his attempts to obscure God's Law. For you who are in Christ, St. Paul says, using military terms, "Stand therefore, having fastened on the belt of truth" (Eph 6:14).

But then comes the next flaming arrow from Satan, the arrow called heartache. He fights you, saying, "Okay, you now may be certain of what you must do—the Ten Commandments—but you do not do them. Therefore, God will not help you. God will not be your God."

Christ, our perfect shield, stops this flaming arrow. Again, in the Sermon on the Mount, He declares: "Do not think that I have come to abolish the Law or the Prophets; I have not come to abolish them but to fulfill them" (Mt 5:17). The Son of God came from heaven and became a man for a reason—to satisfy all God's Law has demanded from you. Jesus obeyed the Ten Commandments perfectly in your place, with His own perfect righteousness. That is the righteousness He now credits to your account through faith in Him.

What a tremendous gift this is! Christ has given you His own perfect righteousness to protect your heart from any heartache, from any failure under God's Law. Christ's righteousness covers it. Again, St. Paul uses military terms. In Christ, "Stand therefore . . . having put on the breastplate of righteousness" (Eph 6:14).

But then comes the third flaming arrow from Satan, called terror. He attacks again, saying, "Okay, Christ may have kept God's Law for you but you still must be punished for your sins. In the end, you'll never have peace, only terror. You will be punished."

Christ, our perfect shield, stops this flaming arrow. The reason Jesus went to the cross was to take the punishment for your sins. After suffering for your sins on Calvary, He looked out and couldn't find any more unpunished sins, so He said, "It is finished!" He took the terror of God's just punishment for your sins and the sins of all so that we might be at peace in Him.

In the waters of Baptism, God washes us clean and gives us this peace. In Holy Absolution those waters continue to flow. With the gift of His peace Christ makes us ready for anything. St. Paul puts it this way, In Christ, "Stand therefore . . . as shoes for your feet, having put on the readiness given by the gospel of peace" (Eph 6:14–15).

The name of Satan's final flaming arrow is hell. His final attack is to argue that, though Christ may have died for you on the cross, death and hell are still stronger than you are. Because you are a sinner, in the end, death and hell will claim you, take you, defeat you.

Christ, our perfect shield, stops this flaming arrow too. Christ rose from the grave, conquering death and hell for you. In His body He visibly ascended into heaven, where He reigns as King of kings and Lord of lords. He has claimed you through faith and Baptism, and He will return to take you home, for you are His. Christ gives you the ultimate protection from the attacks of Satan—salvation— eternal life with Him. In Christ, "Stand therefore . . . and take the helmet of salvation" (Eph 6:14, 17).

In this world, God has given us many good shields: our armed forces, the Patriot missile system, education, family, and friends. But there is only one perfect shield, Jesus Christ, our Lord. He is the only one who can stop and put out the devil's flaming arrows of uncertainty, of heartache, of terror, and of hell. He does this with His truth, His righteousness, His peace, and His salvation as the Son of God. As St. Paul says:

> We do not wrestle against flesh and blood, but against the rulers, against the authorities, against the cosmic powers over this present darkness, against the spiritual forces of evil in the heavenly places. Therefore take up the whole armor of God, that you may be able to withstand in the evil day, and having done all, to stand firm. . . . Take up the shield of faith, with which you can extinguish all the flaming darts of the evil one. (Eph 6:12–13, 16)

Chaplain Jonathan E. Shaw

Thanksgiving Day

Remember to Thank God

Deuteronomy 8:1–10

Today is Thanksgiving Day, a day our nation has set aside to remember to give thanks to our God. In the creation account in the Book of Job we read, "The morning stars sang together and all the sons of God shouted for joy" (38:7). That's the beginning of creation. And in Revelation, the very last book of the Bible, we read of the "elders" who are gathered around the throne of God, praising Him day and night. The Bible in many places speaks of praise to God, from the beginning of creation to the time we're in heaven.

"Give thanks in all circumstances; for this is the will of God in Christ Jesus for you," St. Paul writes (1 Thess 5:18). Praise Him that He is God, first of all. Praise Him that He is the God who through His Son, Jesus Christ, brings life out of death, joy out of sorrow. Praise Him for His presence in those crisis situations of illness and accident, loneliness and death. Praise Him that even though it seems terrible to you at the moment, He is using it as a way of working out His ultimate and good purpose for your life.

Therefore, on this Thanksgiving Day we remember to thank God.

God Wanted Israel to Remember to Thank Him

Here is the new generation, standing on the east bank of the Jordan River, ready to cross over into the land with high anticipation and hope. As Moses is preparing them to enter the land, he encourages them to obey God. God wants them to remember the past and realize that He has been testing and training them.

God tested Israel in the wilderness to humble them, to prove what was really in their hearts, and to teach them (see Deut 8:2–3). Our Lord quoted those verses when He was tempted in the wilderness (Mt 4:4; Lk 4:4).

God has been good to us. He has blessed us in many, many ways, including material blessings, so we might see that there is a spiritual wealth, the Word of God. It is the Word of God that is the real manna for the child of God today.

Deut 8:4 says, "Your foot did not swell these forty years." A missionary doctor explained to me that in the Far East where he served, the people lacked variety in their diet. They did not get all the vitamins they needed, so they showed symptoms of beriberi, including swelling of the feet. The Israelites received all their required vitamins and nourishment through the manna—a miracle food—that God provided. Spiritual manna is the Word of God that supplies all your needs.

And then, the Lord said to the Israelites, "You shall eat and be full, and you shall bless the LORD your God for the good land He has given you" (Deut 8:10). Praise the Lord and thank Him, as all people ought for the food they eat. Even now some people see no reason to thank God for food grown and processed by human hands. Skeptics like to tell of the preacher who complimented a farmer by saying, "You and the Lord produced a fine crop on that field."

"Yes," the farmer replied, "but you should have seen that field when the Lord had it all to Himself. It was nothing but a weed patch."

The skeptics, however, forget what the field would be like if the farmer had it all to himself. All his work would be useless if the Lord did not provide sunshine, rain, and air. Not even weeds would grow without the Lord.

God was calling His people to be thoughtful, not careless. He was urging them to remember Him and all the things that He was doing and how much they depended on Him. How foolish it would be for the people of Israel to forget Him and give themselves all the credit for their success! How foolish it is for people today to do the same!

God Wants Us to Remember to Thank Him

God wants us to remember our past too. Paul put it like this for the believer: "I am sure of this, that He who began a good work in you will bring it to completion at the day of Jesus Christ" (Phil 1:6). We are to remember that God has led us and blessed us in the past and promises to continue to do so in the future. Remembering is for our encouragement.

When our lives are filled with goodness, we begin to feel invincible and, thus, have little need for God. We become neglectful in our praise. In the account of Jesus and the lepers, ten were healed, but only one came back to give praise and thanks. We thank God when Jesus brings His healing power into our lives. It is important that we do not become forgetful and neglectful and self-sufficient in our newfound health and strength.

Thank God for the Gospel!

More than anything else, thank God for the forgiveness of sins, life, and salvation that is ours because of the sacrificial death of His Son, our Lord Jesus Christ.

Jesus' neighbors once chased Him from town and tried to throw Him off a cliff. Jesus' closest friends betrayed and deserted Him in the time of trouble. Jesus' body sweat became blood when He reflected on the sins of the world. Jesus' compassion for the world propelled His broken body up Calvary's hill, where He was executed by order of His own people. Yet through it all Jesus never ceased praising and thanking God. Jesus was the "Sacrifice of Thanksgiving" because He knew the Father would not abandon the world. He knew that after the darkness there would be light; after defeat, victory; after sorrow, joy; after death, resurrection.

Jesus Christ, on the cross, was forsaken by His Father. He suffered agonizing pain for all sin. Finally at the sixth hour, Jesus had completely paid for the sins of the world. He cried from the cross, "It is finished!" But then on Easter Sunday morning He rose. By the resurrection of Jesus Christ we know that God our heavenly Father has accepted the sacrifice of Jesus Christ for our sins. And we know that we, too, will rise from the dead and be with God the Father forever and ever.

Jesus Christ is our heavenly Father's gift for you and for me. Forgiveness of sins is ours! The resurrection is ours! Eternal life in heaven is ours! Remember to thank God for all of this.

Martin Rinckart, author of the hymn "Now Thank We All Our God" (*LSB* 895), lived during the time of the Pilgrims. He lived in a small German village. Unlike the Pilgrims, who journeyed from England to Holland to New England, he was caught in the middle of the Thirty Years' War. Because his village had a big wall around it, thousands of people crammed inside for protection. Adequate sanitation facilities were lacking, as were medical supplies. Food and water supplies became contaminated—conditions not unlike those of the Pilgrims in the belly of the Mayflower. As a result, the plague came. Eight thousand people died during one period of epidemic. For part of this time, Martin Rinckart was the only Christian clergyman in the village. According to his journals, he personally buried more than four thousand bodies—sometimes as many as fifty people in a single day. During this time Rinckart wrote his great hymn:

> Now thank we all our God
> With hearts and hands and voices,
> Who wondrous things has done,
> In whom His world rejoices;
> Who from our mothers' arms
> Has blest us on our way
> With countless gifts of love
> And still is ours today. (*LSB* 895:1)

After the darkness, light; after defeat, victory; after sorrow, joy; after death, resurrection. "I will offer to You the sacrifice of thanksgiving," the psalmist has written (Ps 116:17). Offer to God the praise of sacrifice. Remember to thank God.

Rev. Robert G. Bailey

Thanksgiving Day

The Thanksgiving Journey

Luke 17:11–19

For what are you thankful? Off the top of your head, you may not think of anything. Then again, you might think of many things. Did you think of your body and soul, eyes, ears and all your members, your reason and all your senses? How about clothing and shoes? food and drink? house and home? wife, children, land, or animals? For all these things it is our duty to thank and praise God.[17]

Have you ever done a lot for someone who showed no appreciation? You were probably disappointed. Luke records that an experience like that happened to Jesus. In our Gospel for today, we hear of ten leprous men who were miraculously healed. But only one returned to give Jesus thanks and praise. Jesus asks him, perhaps with a trace of disappointment in His voice, "where are the nine?" (Lk 17:17). How often are we like the other nine, forgetting to say thanks for the wonderful gifts we've received from God? Today, it's only fitting to remember we should give thanks and praise for God's wonderful gifts.

The nine who didn't return to thank Jesus did have faith in Him. They all cried out, "Jesus, master, have mercy on us" (v. 13). This is a prayer for salvation. It's a cry that encompassed all their needs—not just release from leprosy, but release from uncleanness and an end to separation from their families and friends. All ten lepers knew what they needed. They all saw Jesus as their only hope.

Jesus responded to their cry. He told them, "Go and show yourselves to the priests" (v. 14). Jesus sent them to the place where they would be declared clean—released and returned home in every sense. So there's no doubt that all ten men believed in Jesus. With the evidence of disease still visible, they went to show themselves to the priests. On the way, all ten of them were healed of their leprosy. There's no doubt that all of them rejoiced and were happy about what happened to them.

But only one of them remembered who it was that had healed them. One of them, an outsider to the Jewish people—a Samaritan—saw the God of creation at work in his own life. This one leper saw God in this man, Jesus of Nazareth, and returned to give thanks and praise to that God. He rejoiced not only in the healing of his sin but also in a healing that made him part of a community again. He was now reconciled to God, forgiven of his sins, and given a new life. This Samaritan

---

18 Paraphrased from *Luther's Small Catechism*, pp. 15–16.

leper's prayer for salvation, "Jesus, Master, have mercy on us," is fully answered. Jesus tells the man to leave his worship and continue in the journey of faith. He tells him, "Rise and go your way; your faith has made you well" (v. 19). The salvation he prayed for is now his.

Today, many people are giving thanks for material blessings. Even people who normally have little or nothing to do with God will invoke His name and say, "Thank You." But once this National Day of Thanksgiving is over, will they continue thanking God? Maybe they'll remember God in some time of personal, family, or national crisis. But then again, maybe not. Even you and I sometimes find ourselves weak when it comes to thanking and praising God. We tend to be better askers than thankers. "God, please perform for us! Feed us! Smooth things out! Defend us against our enemies! Make us happy!" Too often we presume God's promise to feed us. We ask for our daily bread but often forget to thank God when we get it, day in and day out.

And we do have lots of reasons to give thanks! Consider again the ten lepers from the Gospel. Jesus healed all ten of them of an incurable disease. But only the Samaritan recognized the Healer behind the healing. Only one of the ten recognized the Giver behind the gift. He believed not only that God had healed him but also that this God was Jesus of Nazareth. The foreigner believed and returned to thank and praise. Thanksgiving flowed into worship.

Jesus may not have healed us from leprosy, but He has healed us from something infinitely greater. Jesus Christ died for us on the cross to deliver us from the diseases of sin, of death, and of the devil. You and I who suffer from the mortal disease of sin have been healed. In the waters of Baptism, the forgiveness won by Christ on His cross was applied to each of us. God called us by name, set us on the journey of faith, and healed us. That's more than enough reason to thank and praise God!

That thanks and praise flows out in worship. Today, we gather in worship around God's Word and the Sacrament we sometimes call "Eucharist." *Eucharist* is nothing other than the Greek word for "thanksgiving." We gather on Thanksgiving Day because our president issued a proclamation to do so in our respective houses of worship. We're thankful to have this time to thank God for giving us a good government. We give thanks for all the good gifts God has bestowed on us this year. In gratitude to God, "supplications, prayers, intercessions, and thanksgivings [are to] be made for all people, for kings and all who are in high positions, that we may lead a peaceful and quiet life, godly and dignified in every way" (1 Tim 2:1–2).

So for what are we thankful? There's almost too much to count! All our material blessings; the privilege of having been made children of God and heirs of heaven; living in a nation with rule of law and freedom, especially the freedom to worship the one true God. These are all gifts we have received and continue to enjoy. Thanks and praise to God in Jesus Christ!

As God healed the ten lepers, so does He give good gifts to the thankful and unthankful alike. As the thankful who have returned to offer thanks and praise, we praise God for the faith that enables us to thank Him for all His blessings. "Oh give thanks to the LORD, for He is good; for His steadfast love endures forever!" (Ps 118:29). We give thanks not only today but also every day as we journey through this life on the road of thanksgiving as recipients of God's wonderful gifts.

Rev. John-Paul Meyer

Thanksgiving Day

To Be Content: Four Options

Philippians 4:10–13

Years ago a woman from the former Soviet Union visited New York. She was not too impressed by what she saw. She said Moscow also had a large airport and a magnificent subway system. But when she was taken into a supermarket, she stopped, looked around, and simply broke down and cried.

I think of that woman and people in other countries where there is a shortage of food. Then I think of how discontented I sometimes feel when I cannot find the exact brand of food I want in the supermarket. It makes me feel sheepish, to say the least. I feel even worse when, though living in the lap of plenty, I become envious of what others have.

Here it is Thanksgiving. We all want to be happy, and most of us are; but too often our joys are tinged with apprehension. Will our happiness end before the day is out? That phone ringing—I hope it isn't an accident; I hope they're just late. I wonder if someone here today won't be here next Thanksgiving. I would truly be happy if only . . . . Are we so dependent on circumstances that we cannot be content for longer than a short while?

In today's Epistle, we are looking at part of a thank-you letter that the apostle Paul wrote to the Philippians. Believe it or not, he was in prison or under house arrest when he wrote, "I have learned in whatever situation I am to be content. I know how to be brought low, and I know how to abound" (Phil 4:11–12). If we are to be content, we have to be prepared to accept both good and bad, often in quick succession. How do we do that?

A woman came to her pastor with a problem that is common but usually is not expressed. Her husband had recently bought a small business. After the first ten months, business blossomed beyond their expectations. "I have a strange feeling. Don't smile at me, but I almost think I should feel guilty."

"Why?" asked the pastor.

"I don't think that we deserve it," she answered, "and I don't think we have earned it."

He thought for a moment and counseled her, "If business is up, thank God. You could sing 'Now thank we all our God.' And when business is down, you could sing the Kyrie, 'Lord, have mercy on us.' God walks with you in both situations."

There are three common ways I have observed in which people try to be content.

"If I make enough money and invest it wisely, I should have more financial security, so at least I won't have to worry about money. Then I can be reasonably content." Few people would argue with that, but financial security is not a secure foundation for contentment. In the parable of the sower, Jesus warned about the danger of "the cares and riches and pleasures of life" choking out our relationship with God (Lk 8:14).

When you think of the pressure of always wanting more, you can understand the popularity of a book like *When All You Have Is Not Good Enough*. It is by an insightful rabbi, Harold Kushner, based on his understanding of Ecclesiastes.

"If I could just think more positively, improve my self-image, be more assertive, and learn how to get other people to do what I want, I would be able to take control of my life, feel good about myself, believe in myself, and achieve what I want. Then I'll be content." But if this is your way of seeking contentment, you must ask, "Can I really change myself for the better?" And other questions arise: "Am I seeking happiness at the expense of others? What price do I pay for contentment?"

Some people think they'll be content if they can just escape the whirl of activity and responsibility. "Stop the world; I want to get off." There's too much competition, and it's too confusing. Perhaps they're exhausted. They seek contentment by sitting on the sidelines. But doing so reduces the possibility of sharing God-given gifts and talents with others who need them and of finding the joy that comes from helping others. There is no real contentment in passivity, is there?

I suppose we all have experimented with these options from time to time. But discontentment is a deeply spiritual problem. It afflicts rich and poor alike. We may not want to admit we suffer from it. We may prefer to ignore it. But for most of us, it is a recurring problem, eating away at our souls and robbing us of joy.

Yet there is a fourth option—another source of contentment, which is described in our text. Where did the apostle find contentment? In the fact that he was forgiven, justified by God because of Jesus Christ, who died on the cross to forgive all his sins. For this reason, the apostle Paul had peace with God—a peace that surpassed all human understanding, a peace that did not depend in the least upon his circumstances in life.

If we are discontented, it may mean that we have become disconnected from God, that we are not at peace with Him. We are connected to God through faith in His Son. "Since we have been justified by faith, we have peace with God through our Lord Jesus Christ" (Rom 5:1).

We heard in the first part of the Epistle for today, "The peace of God, which surpasses all understanding, will guard your hearts and your minds in Christ Jesus" (v. 7). This peace is not just a mood or something we talk ourselves into. It is the forgiveness and reconciliation with God that Christ has provided at great cost. This peace guards us and protects us. We all need a guardian of peace to accompany us through the twists and turns of life.

Here is what Paul wrote to Timothy about peaceful contentment: "Now there is great gain in godliness with contentment, for we brought nothing into the world, and we cannot take anything out of the world. But if we have food and clothing, with these we will be content. But those who desire to be rich fall into temptation, into a snare, into many senseless and harmful desires that plunge people into ruin and destruction. For the love of money is a root of all kinds of evils. It is through this craving that some have wandered away from the faith and pierced themselves with many pangs" (1 Tim 6:6–10).

The apostle was content because he had learned the sufficiency of God's grace. Do you remember how Paul felt about his "thorn in the flesh?" Three times he pleaded with God to take it away, but the Lord said to him, "My grace is sufficient for you, for My power is made perfect in weakness" (2 Cor 12:9).

The power of God to save is found in the weakness of Christ crucified for us. Paul learned to be content even though he often suffered, because he trusted in the Savior who suffered for him. So Paul could say, "Therefore I will boast all the more gladly of my weaknesses, so that the power of Christ may rest upon me. For the sake of Christ, then, I am content with weaknesses, insults, hardships, persecutions, and calamities. For when I am weak, then I am strong" (2 Cor 12:9–10).

This contentment, this inner peace, led him to say, "I can do all things through Him [Christ] who strengthens me" (Phil 4:13). Certain of Christ's gracious presence, His strength enables us to resist temptation, to overcome anger, to forgive, to reach out, to make peace, to outlast evil, to be renewed, to survive, and to love again. "I have learned in whatever situation I am to be content" (Phil 4:11), we heard from the apostle Paul.

One of the most beautiful expressions of Christian contentment came from the pen of the hymn writer Horatio Spafford. He lost his family in a sailing voyage across the Atlantic to Europe. It must have taken great determination and love for him to later make the same voyage. But he came to terms with his God and his grief when he wrote these lines:

> When peace, like a river, attendeth my way;
> When sorrows, like sea billows, roll;
> Whatever my lot, Thou hast taught me to say,
> It is well, it is well with my soul. (*LSB* 763:1)

When the soul finds rest in Christ, there is peace, contentment, and strength to deal with anything life may bring. Having Christ, we have all we will ever need. Peace be with you this Thanksgiving.

Rev. Paul E. Schuessler

New Year's Eve

The Numbering of Our Days

Psalm 90

> Teach us all to number our days, that we may apply our hearts unto wisdom and finally be saved. (traditional prayer for the bereaved)

On April 15, 1912, E. J. Smith, the captain of a large passenger liner, led the passengers of his ship in a Sunday morning devotion. The worship service included the singing of the familiar hymn "O God, Our Help in Ages Past," which includes the words:

> Time, like an ever-rolling stream,
> Soon bears us all away;
> We fly forgotten as a dream
> Dies at the op'ning day. (*LSB* 733:5)

About sixteen hours after the service, 1,502 people from among the passengers and crew of that ship learned firsthand the meaning of those words as the *Titanic* slowly sank beneath the waves of the North Atlantic. That hymn, along with Psalm 90, upon which the hymn is based, bears vivid witness to the swift passage of time and the shortness of human life, facts that are already on our minds as the year *(year)* quickly fades into *(year)*.

How short life is! In times of trouble and hardship the days may seem to stretch on forever and ever, but when we look back upon the days gone by, we still must exclaim, "How short life is!" Despite all our avoidance strategies, we are always confronted by the stark reality of this truth: "we fly away" (v. 10), and so quickly that we are soon forgotten as a dream. Many of us cannot recite the full names of our own grandparents, the very people who mean so much to our parents, who in turn mean so much to us. Unless the end of the world comes first, even the cemetery memorial stones, which will supposedly mark our whereabouts forever, will soon weather away and be erased. In the psalm before us, Moses, who has seen a whole generation of his Israelite brothers and sisters die during a forty-year span in the wilderness, faces the prospect of his own death. He speaks of human life as something quickly washed away by a torrential rain, as a sleep that is over even before we become aware of the passage of time, and as grass that is mowed down the same day it first sprang up. All people return to the dust from whence they came. In the psalm, Moses uses the word *we* to emphasize that not even the people of God are exempt from the swift race toward death.

As the passage of life is swift, so also death is inevitable, no matter what people do to try to masquerade its inevitability. Some of us will try to hide from death through sheer busyness. We figure that as long as we are occupied with a multitude of duties and hobbies, we will not have the time even to think about death. Others of us will stock up on so many of the world's supplies that we can thereby pretend that we are never going to leave this world behind. Still others will think that we can push back the inevitable indefinitely through special diets and fitness programs. Some try to insulate themselves from death by institutionalizing it, tucking it away behind the solid brick walls of hospitals and funeral chapels. There will always be those who try to "immortalize" themselves, those who by sheer effort and achievement attempt to leave in this world a permanent mark that no one could possibly forget. And finally, there will be those who try to philosophize death away by adopting an "eat, drink, and be merry" outlook, or by viewing death through rose-colored glasses as simply a return to Mother Nature.

But through Moses, the "man of God," the Lord Almighty exposes the whole masquerade. Go ahead! Shout and laugh and cry and sweat and squirm and rationalize as you will, the brick wall is still there, and it stops everyone cold in his or her tracks. The sand in the hourglass will not slow down for anyone. Threescore and ten—seventy years, perhaps eighty, but not much more than that. Even after a whole life of scurrying about, your long list of accomplishments, the things that cause you to burst with pride, will amount to nothingness or, at most, the sweat that accumulated on your brow.

As generation follows upon generation, what is it that makes the human situation so helpless and hopeless? Here Moses remains relentless in his honest appraisal of life in this world. The entire problem from beginning to end, the problem that always was and now is, belongs not with God, but with us. The problem has always been our sin and guilt—sin that is nothing less than the cause of humanity's mortality. Even our secret sins are totally laid bare in God's presence. We have built up the brick wall of death with our own hands, but our hands are entirely powerless to tear that wall down again. If we could double our anticipated lifespan, we would probably be driven mad by living so long in a world as sinful as ours.

And so it is that Moses simply will not tolerate any false optimism about human life. So-called positive attitudes about life and pondering the possibilities of life are exposed for what they are. He would have us look at human life with such complete honesty that we despair of it entirely. As we stare death in the face, and examine all the problems that lead up to it, we can do no more than fall flat on our faces.

However, Moses wants us to fall flat on our faces in the right direction—in worship of God. He does not leave us comfortless. Already in the first verse of the psalm, he shows us the direction in which he wants us to fall: "Lord, You have been our dwelling place in all generations" (v. 1).

What is the answer, the solution, to the human dilemma? In the spirit of the psalmist, we confess, "O Lord, the answer to our poverty is not wealth. The answer to our sicknesses is not health. The answer to our sadness is not our happiness. The answer to everything that life and death can throw at us is You, and You alone."

As expected, never in this psalm does Moses blame God for the problems we have brought upon ourselves. But there is something incredibly enlightening about this psalm. Moses does not base his evaluation of human life on either a false optimism or on pessimism. Whether he was feeling good or bad, he simply draws a comparison, a contrast, between us transitory humans and our eternal God. In other words, what we happen to think or feel is not what counts. What really matters is what God thinks and feels and does for us.

With this in mind, Moses speaks for all of us when he prays, "Return, O LORD! . . . Have pity on Your servants!" (v. 13). It is that compassion, that mercy, that makes all the difference in the world. Like the mountains He created, His steadfast love was there for us long before we were born, and it will be there for us when we die. His mercy has been shown and given to us in the person of His Son, Jesus Christ.

The Lord Jesus came into this world knowing what He would find. He experienced the full range of life's problems (though without sin). In Gethsemane, He stared death in the face, and alone on Calvary, He slammed into death's brick wall and shattered it. By His death He has destroyed death, and He has opened the kingdom of heaven to all believers. The prayer of Moses, "Satisfy us in the morning with Your steadfast love" (v. 14), was answered on Easter morning when Jesus arose on the other side of the wall as our conquering Lamb.

Our own grandchildren may forget our names. The stones that mark our resting places may be obliterated or removed. But when we are baptized into the death of our Lord Jesus, we are also baptized into His resurrection. By His grace, we count for something. We are not forgotten; He remembers our baptismal name. Our life with Christ is described so beautifully by Moses: "Teach us to number our days that we may get a heart of wisdom" (v. 12). There are three ways in which we count our days as children of God. First, we count our days to be reminded of our human frailty. The days, months, and years that fly by continually remind us of our sinful condition and that God, and only God, can remove our despair over it.

Second, we count the days by a brand-new unit of measurement: we count them not by days and months and years, but by the grace of God. Each day we behold with wonder the mercies of God, which are new every morning. Gone are our frantic efforts toward self-preservation. Gone are our blind efforts to masquerade the stark fact of our own mortality. Gone are our attempts to put our name on the map to be remembered. It is what He has done that counts, and in His salvation we find perfect peace. We can say, "Let the days and years roll by! My days will be as limitless as His mercy. My name is written in the Lamb's Book of Life. The answers to all my woes are the one answer, the Lord Jesus Christ. My desire is to be with Christ, for that is far better. Come quickly, Lord Jesus!"

And third, we count each day because each day is precious in the eyes of God. Each day is a precious opportunity to serve our Redeemer, to do the works that He has prepared beforehand that we should walk in them. Moses says it rightly: even now God establishes the works of our hands. We will be remembered for the works God performs through us; these works, the apostle John tells us, will follow us into eternal life.

The apostle Paul had a great way of putting together all these different ways of numbering our days. He said to the Church in Corinth, "We were so utterly burdened beyond our strength that we despaired of life itself. Indeed, we felt that we had received the sentence of death. But that was to make us rely not on ourselves but on God who raises the dead" (2 Cor 1:8–9). The very same apostle said to the Church at Philippi, "If I am to live in the flesh, that means fruitful labor for me" (Phil 1:22). As a child of God, Paul valued life in this world so much that he could not decide whether he wanted to remain on earth to labor for Christ or be with Christ in glory.

As children of God we can number our days in a similar fashion. We can get up in the morning, observe the continuous ticking of our alarm clock, flip over another page on our calendar, and thank God that we are very much remembered by Him, since we have been baptized in His triune name. As people who have been baptized into both the death and resurrection of Jesus Christ, we can say a twofold prayer: "Lord, please take me out of this sinful, dead-end place called the world. But until You do, Lord, I thank You for each joyous day under Your mercy. Help me to relish every moment of life here that You give me."

Rev. James G. Bollhagen

New Year's Eve

Are You Better Off Now?

Isaiah 51:1–6

Are you better off tonight than you were 365 days ago? To answer this question, you may need to consult with several people.

Your accountant would be able to help you determine your current financial condition, compared with what it was at this time last year. By simple comparison, you would know whether your net worth had increased or decreased.

Your doctor would be your best resource to determine your physical condition. By performing a thorough examination, your doctor could tell you the general condition of your heart and circulatory system, lungs and respiratory system, stomach and digestive system, and the rest of your bodily organs and functions.

Through your annual performance evaluation, your boss would tell you how you have performed at work. You will learn whether you are a valued employee or if your employment future is on shaky ground. You might be told certain improvements must be made to keep your job.

Some of you sitting here this evening may not have evaluated the past year. Yet there is a sense within you regarding where you are tonight compared with one year ago. Some of you certainly feel good about this past year. Others are ambivalent. Still others are concerned. And some are on the verge of despair.

How Shall We Evaluate Our Lives?

But consider these amazing statements. Some people whom the general public would call "dirt poor" feel quite good about themselves. They are satisfied with life. Some individuals with terminal medical conditions or chronic illnesses feel positive about the past year as well as the future. Some of those who did not receive a job promotion or salary increase believe they have the best job in the world.

As we end this year and begin the new, we might want to evaluate our lives based on net worth, health condition, position at work, or some other earthly criteria. Our text, however, offers another method for evaluating our life. Isaiah challenges us to consider what we put our faith and trust in. He writes: "Listen to me, you who pursue righteousness, you who seek the LORD" (51:1).

Isaiah describes what needs to be foundational in our Christian life—the pursuit of righteousness, seeking after the Lord. We don't do this on our own, somehow choosing to seek God. No, Isaiah beautifully brings out in our text that we pursue righteousness and seek the Lord because of what God has done in us and for us in the person of Jesus Christ.

God's Grace and Mercy

This passage in Isaiah reminds us of God's great miraculous work, calling to our attention the many ways God's grace and mercy impact our lives. In v. 2, Isaiah takes us back to Abraham and Sarah, who were beyond childbearing years; yet, by the power of God, they conceived and bore a child. As we consider this miracle, we are reminded that our membership in God's family is by His grace and goodness. We are well-off tonight—spiritually speaking—because God had mercy on a man named Abraham. God chose to give him faith, chose to give him a child he should never have fathered, chose to make his descendants number like the stars, chose to bring from his descendants the Savior of the world.

In v. 3, God comforted and showed compassion to Zion, even when Zion had forsaken Him. The last two verses of our text make it crystal clear that it was God's saving work that redeemed and restored Israel as His family. "My righteousness draws near, My salvation has gone out, and My arms will judge the peoples. . . . My salvation will be forever, and My righteousness will never be dismayed" (vv. 5–6).

So many individuals, including the Jewish people of Jesus' day, interpret God's promises to comfort and restore His people to mean earthly power, wealth, and prestige. Sadly, even some Christians misunderstand the biblical concepts of restoration and comfort. God's promises give us strength. God's promise of forgiveness of sins through faith in His Son comforts us. God's promises, fulfilled through His Son, Jesus, assure us of an eternal victory over all the forces of evil.

St. Paul so eloquently states the Christian's position in Romans 8: "If God is for us, who can be against us? He who did not spare His own Son but gave Him up for us all, how will He not also with Him graciously give us all things?" (vv. 31–32).

All Begins with God's Love

Our well-being begins with God's love for us in Christ Jesus, as the prophet writes, "My salvation will be forever, and My righteousness will never be dismayed" (v. 6). This Gospel message gives us assurance. This Gospel message gives us strength to endure what comes our way every day, month, and year. This Gospel message enables us to be positive even if our net worth went down, our health deteriorated, or our employment went sour.

"I am sure that neither death nor life, nor angels nor rulers, nor things present nor things to come, nor powers, nor height nor depth, nor anything else in all creation, will be able to separate us from the love of God in Christ Jesus our Lord"

(Rom 8:38–39). God gave a son to an aged couple. God caused His own Son to be born of a virgin. God, in love, sacrificed His own Son on the cross of Calvary for your forgiveness and life. This God helps us endure hardships and disappointments. He helps us endure any difficulty.

"Give attention to Me, My people, and give ear to Me, My nation; for a law will go out from Me, and I will set My justice for a light to the peoples" (v. 4). The word *law* here does not mean the Ten Commandments but the pronouncement of our need for a Savior and the fulfillment of God's salvation plan in Jesus Christ. It is a Gospel pronouncement that points us to God's love for sinners. It assures us that God desires to save all people from their sins. God's Good News is salvation for all people in the person and work of His Son, Jesus Christ.

"For the LORD comforts Zion; He comforts all her waste places and makes her wilderness like Eden, her desert like the garden of the LORD; joy and gladness will be found in her, thanksgiving and the voice of song" (v. 3). The Lord still gives His people the strength to live as His people. The Lord still gives His people faith to trust in His grace and mercy. The Lord still forgives His people their sins as they repent and seek His forgiveness through Jesus Christ.

By God's grace, we are present at this worship service. We have passed through another year because God has enabled us to do so. Despite our financial, physical, or employment status, we are blessed people because of God's bountiful provision. God meets our every spiritual need through the power of the Gospel, through the daily renewal of His baptismal grace, and through the body and blood of Jesus, which we receive through the Sacrament of the Altar.

Are we better off tonight than we were 365 days ago? The answer is no! We are still the same sinful residents of a fallen world. But we are the redeemed children of God, thankful to have received God's grace and mercy every day this past year. And it is by God's grace that we can say we are equally well-off tonight as we were last year or ten years ago because God's salvation will last forever; His righteousness will never fail.

Rev. Ray G. Mirly

New Year's Eve

He the Source, the Ending He

Galatians 4:4–7

THE RELEVANCY AND RELATIVITY OF TIME

It should come as no surprise that on New Year's Eve the subject of time gets center stage. Tonight, when the clock strikes midnight, we end one year and begin another, a new 365 days.

That time is relevant, of enormous impact, is beyond debate. Often it dictates when we eat, sleep, work, and play. Many of us are inordinately dependent on our clocks and wristwatches to get us through the day. On the other hand, time is also relative, depending on one's perspective and situation in life. There are those who have much too much time on their hands and the moments of each day pass at a snail's pace: the lonely, the isolated, the imprisoned, the fearful, the invalid and infirm, the depressed.

By contrast, there are those who believe they have all the time in the world: time to pursue their dreams, to raise their families, to build their nest eggs, and, sadly, to order their spiritual lives. An older person in one of our congregation's Bible classes observed that people seem to be more involved in Bible study later in life, when they "have more time." Unfortunately, she may be right. But she is also wrong. We all have the same amount of time each day, each week, each year. The patterns and priorities we set for ourselves for the way we use our time in the prime of life provide a context for how we spend our time later in life. Most of us find time for whatever is important to us—whatever we consider of value.

Somewhere between those who have too much time and those who believe they have all the time in the world are those who have no time—those who are pulled in many different directions, each of which requires time: vocation, leisure, marriage, family, church. These find special comfort in the psalmist's words, "The LORD will keep your going out and your coming in from this time forth and forevermore" (Ps 121:8). This is comforting especially when we find ourselves "coming and going," not knowing where or how or when to expend our priorities.

Thus, during these last hours of *(year)*, we take time to place time into the timetable of our timeless God.

The Eternal God Enters into Time

Our text is Gal 4:4–7: "But when the fullness of time had come, God sent forth His Son, born of woman, born under the law, to redeem those who were under the law, so that we might receive adoption as sons. And because you are sons, God has sent the Spirit of His Son into our hearts, crying, 'Abba! Father!' So you are no longer a slave, but a son, and if a son, then an heir through God."

"When the fullness of time had come . . ." With God, nothing is haphazard or happenstance. God has a time for everything, and everything God plans happens on time, especially God's plan for our redemption. So it was that almost two thousand years ago, God decided that it was time—the right time, the fullness of time—for the Savior to be born—a timeless God entering a time-driven world.

Why then? Why not years earlier? Why didn't God send a Savior to deliver His chosen people from Egyptian oppression? Because, perhaps, one and a half millennia later when the Savior did come, God's people were under a more insidious form of slavery—one with eternal consequences. They had become subject to the expectations and exploitations of religious leaders such as the Pharisees, who exulted themselves as exemplars of the faith, who deluded others into believing that their self-serving piety pleased God, whose religion became synonymous with rituals and rites and the rigidity of rules.

There is no greater bondage of our will and spirit than seeking to satisfy God. There is no greater spiritual enslavement than to believe that we are in charge of our eternal destiny. If, even for a split second, we believe that our relationship with the Lord and the fate of our salvation is dependent on the type of person we are—what kind of father or mother, husband or wife, pastor or plumber; how good or effective or productive or kind—we would be more oppressed than the lowliest, most subservient slave.

That's why the Father sent the Son into the world in the fullness of time, namely, to redeem us from the curse and burden of the Law and to place it squarely on the shoulders of Jesus. He, born of a woman—fully human and fully divine—was also born "under" the Law. He kept the Law perfectly—not the superficial mandates penned by the Pharisees—but the letter and spirit of God's holy, piercing, and penetrating Law. It is impossible for us to keep the Law. We can't even get past the First Commandment, "You shall have no other gods," let alone the other nine without saying *mea culpa*—I plead guilty! Christ's keeping of the Law is an imperative part of His act of salvation.

Even that was not sufficient to meet the criteria established by God for our salvation. The only Son of the Father also had to pay the price of sin's consequence! And so He did, on the cross of Calvary, taking our sins upon Himself, literally and spiritually dying our death.

As we know and believe and confess, our sin and His death could not hold Him as a slave in bondage. Aha, Easter! Resurrection! New life! And through Christ's holy life, sacrificial death, and powerful resurrection, we are called sons and daughters of almighty God. We have been given the incredible invitation to call the God who created time in the first place, "*Abba*, Father," "Dear Father." For if we are God's children, then we are also God's heirs, heirs of life forever in heaven.

This message is simple and straightforward Law and Gospel, sin and grace, bondage and freedom, and it is supremely relevant for all generations, for all years, for all time. For it transforms the temporal into the eternal. It puts into heavenly perspective everything with which we concern ourselves during this brief time that we are citizens on earth. Frankly, I can't conceive of a more appropriate way to conclude one year and invite a new one than with the assurance that we are God's children, beloved of the Father.

HE THE SOURCE, THE ENDING HE

This sermon's theme is a line in a hymn normally sung throughout Christmastide, yet appropriate for all seasons. It takes our speck of life here on earth and places it within the framework of the unimaginable, incomprehensible expanse of God.

> Of the Father's love begotten
> Ere the worlds began to be,
> He is Alpha and Omega,
> He the source, the ending He,
> Of the things that are, that have been,
> And that future years shall see
> Evermore and evermore. (*LSB* 384:1)

"He the source, the ending He" of life itself. Christ the Lord has been with us since before we were born and shall be with us when our time on this earth comes to an end. And for certain, Christ is with us now at year's end and year's beginning. Actually, there is no ending for our lives, for—remember—we inherit eternity. Yet as we reflect and ponder the year now ending, on past decades, even on all our life, we see the hand of God upon us. A rhetorical, yet spiritual and relevant question: Can we dare enter a new year without an ever-deepening relationship with the eternal Christ?

"He the source, the ending He" of love itself. There is no greater love than that which the Father gives us through the Son. There is no greater love than that which receives us and welcomes us, not on our terms, but through God's grace and mercy. That we are the children of God and may call upon God in the most endearing of terms, "*Abba,* Father," is not what we merit but is a profound show of God's love.

"He the source, the ending He" of what is, what has been, and what will be, "evermore and evermore."

Rev. Steven H. Albers